THE MOUNTAIN GIANTS

First published in 1993 by Absolute Classics, an imprint of
Absolute Press, 14 Widcombe Crescent, Bath, England

Cover and text design: Ian Middleton

Typesetting by Font U Like, Bath

Printed by The Longdunn Press Ltd, Bristol

ISBN 0 948230 62 2

THE MOUNTAIN GIANTS

Luigi Pirandello

a new version by
Charles Wood

b s o l u t e   c l a s s i c s

INTRODUCTION

When I told a playwright of my old acquaintance I was going to do a version of Pirandello's THE MOUNTAIN GIANTS, he brayed, "Money for old rope!"

Well, not much money and not much rope either, just enough to toss over a beam and do the usual with, but he had a point though he didn't know it because he didn't know the play - which is the most complex and vivid exploration of the use of imagination and the shoddiness of our means of expressing that imagination I have come across among other things, a lot of other things, and it is so brilliantly written that an adaptation or ' version' is simply a process of uncovering meaning and presenting it in speakable English; a process one can never be sure is finished with when preparing a play for the stage.

Like all plays with real guts, light shines at an unexpected moment and something dense as treacle becomes clear as spring water to smiles of relief, gratitude and absorption.

A ' version' starts off the process but when rehearsing stubborn bits there is inevitably recourse to the original text in Italian or literal translation (a furtive look at a crib) before taking a chance on my ' version' being right. This is when the hemp dangles ominously, because I am just as likely to be wrong, especially as Pirandello didn't finish the play; he died before properly starting on the last act or scene.

He said how he thought it might come out. He knew what was to happen to his characters. He knew the pass he had brought them to.

What he didn't get to do is go back over the play in the light of his last act, something most writers do, removing the false starts, red herrings, passages going nowhere, wind taken out of sails by squalls elsewhere. I don't know enough about Pirandello to know how he worked and it is possible his last act would have come forth as a consequence of *every* word and action gone before, but it's unlikely. There will be things within the play mean nothing at all, left there for their intrinsic worth.

There was a skip on the floor for rehearsals and on the basketwork was painted "NT" and "TNP", not important, but the labels said that it was a theatrical skip, costumes, properties and to me it was an exciting and significant object, my eyes kept going to it. I knew what was in it - everything.

When I was a boy we had a skip like it, all actors did, and when my father and mother went off during the war without it, I pillaged it, pulled it apart, disembowelled it, nose deep into its stuff smell, sweat and greasepaint, leather, dust, size and dirty cloth - sequins have a smell, and feathers, and the fur of a busby, and a dead mouse.

I don't suppose I've got THE MOUNTAIN GIANTS right, but I've pulled everything out and tried to explain what it is I've discovered matters for me, in a last act which cannot ever be the last act Pirandello had in mind.

It could end as Toscanini did when he conducted TURANDOT, unfinished by Puccini; a tap of his baton and "Here the master died!"

CHARLES WOOD
June 1993

THE MOUNTAIN GIANTS was first performed in this translation at the National Theatre in 1993. The cast was as follows:

The Inhabitants of the Villa Scalogna:

COTRONE, known as the magician	Desmond Barrit
QUAQUEO, the dwarf	Martin Chamberlain
DUCCIO DOCCIA	Mitch Webb
LA SGRICIA	Eve Pearce
MILORDINO	William Cox
MARA-MARA known also as the Scotswoman	Maggie McCarthy

The Contessa's Company:

ILSE, also known as the Contessa	Sian Thomas
THE COUNT, her husband	Mark Tandy
DIAMANTE, the second female lead	Jennie Stoller
CROMO, the character actor	Philip Locke
SPIZZI, the juvenile lead	Joss Brook
BATTAGLIA, the female impersonator	Christopher Campbell
SACERDOTE	Robin Sneller
LUMACHI, who draws the cart	Howard Ward
MARIA MADDALENA	Buddug Morgan
ANGEL OF THE CENTURY OF GOD	Robin Sneller
FIRST NEIGHBOUR	Sonya Leite
SECOND NEIGHBOUR	Sandra Freeman
CUCCORULLO, a civil servant	Brian Lipson
SMALL MAN	Mitch Webb
PUPPETS	William Cox, Buddug Morgan
SAILOR PUPPET	Jack Murphy

DIRECTOR	William Gaskill
DESIGNER	Annie Smart
LIGHTING	Andy Phillips
MUSIC	Adrian Johnston

ACT ONE

Scene: villa called "La Scalogna". Italy. 1937. Dusk.

A villa which may be hanging to the rock slide of a mountain rising up from the waters of a lake. There may be balconies, steps, doors, balustrades, columns and domes, trees. Possibly a low branched cypress. Green splash of grass, herbs and mountain flowers form an apron which invites performance. The villa and its tumbling seignorial grandeur are like the relaxed embrace of the arms of a crumbled amphitheatre. Music, strange and leaping. Shrieks of apprehensive song. The tension of something about to happen.

Discovered in the villa - still as the stone or moulded plaster until they speak - Quaqueo, La Sgricia, Duccio Doccia and Milordino, quondam variety artists stranded by choice in once opulent digs. When the music stops there is silence until Milordino calls out in alarm:

MILORDINO: Alarm ! Help ! People ! There is somebody coming ... there are people coming ... stand to in the villa ! Alaaaaaaaaaarm !

                Milordino is an unshaven emaciated young man, juggler, eccentric dancer, trick cyclist, chronically and permanently tired - covered in mould from his bowler hat to his pumps. Dignity lives in his once resplendent doublet, now rotten.

                La Sgricia scurries into life.

LA SGRICIA: Who ! Where, where ? *(Into the villa she calls.)* Quick ! Help ! Somebody coming ... people ...

                La Sgricia is a perpetually irritated old woman in bonnet, violet cape, black and white check dress and net mittens. Wrinkled, with cunning lively eyes, she is peasant, wife, landlady, mother-in-law, the cane wielding headmistress of countless sketches and she believes she is dead.

MILORDINO: Lots of them ...

LA SGRICIA: Lots of them ... do you hear me ?

MILORDINO: Alarm ... help !

DOCCIA: Stand to ! Stand to ...

QUAQUEO: Don't worry ... they're lost ...

> *Quaqueo is tiny, round, childlike, big red cheeks,*
> *red hair, a roly-poly foolishly smiling knockabout*
> *comic with steel of malice in his eyes.*

MILORDINO: No they're not ...

LA SGRICIA: Alarm, alarm, alarm ... !

> *Quaqueo clambering up to Milordino.*

QUAQUEO: It's dark and they're lost ... calm down ...

LA SGRICIA: How many ?

QUAQUEO: ... silly buggers, lost ...

MILORDINO: Ten, or more ...

QUAQUEO: Give them the green tongue. That'll scare them off
                ... where ?

LA SGRICIA: *(Calling into the villa)* Quick ! The green tongue ...
                quick, thunder and lightning ... alarm !

DOCCIA: Hold on, hold on ... lightning costs the earth.

> *Duccio Doccia is pale, bald, of uncertain age,*
> *lugubrious, with serious egg shaped eyes and a*
> *pendulous lower lip - a straight man, accountant,*
> *penitent, beggar. His posture is that of someone for*
> *ever just about to sit.*

LA SGRICIA: There's ten of them ... alarm !

Flames of green fire lick the air.

QUAQUEO: It's all right, they're lost ...

MILORDINO: They're not ... they're not lost. They're coming here.

QUAQUEO: *(Frightened, agreeing)* He's right ... they're not lost, do something !

LA SGRICIA: Lightning ... !

DOCCIA: *(In monetary anguish)* Yes ... yes ... but it costs the earth you know ... *(Lightning - Doccio winces in resignation)*... does lightning.

MILORDINO: *(Loud and urgent whisper)* There is a woman in a hand-cart.

QUAQUEO: I see her. She's dead, no she's moving, on the cart arms and legs out she ...

MILORDINO: *(Tugging at him)* Sssssssssh ... they'll hear you !

QUAQUEO: *(Loud whisper)*... moves ... she moves she does, she moves ...

LA SGRICIA: Mara-mara ! Set Mara-mara on them.

DOCCIA: *(Urgently into the villa)* Mara-mara ! Where are you?

MILORDINO: One pulls, two push ...

DOCCIA: Mara-mara !

LA SGRICIA: Mara-mara !

> *Enter Mara-mara from the villa to a fart of bagpipes and a flash of lightning. She is a small overstuffed doll of a woman in tartan, armed with a parasol which she wields like rifle and bayonet when she does not twirl it coquettishly.*

| MARA-MARA: | *(Ludicrous accent)* Och aye the noo ! *(Parasol on guard)* Let me at 'em ! Set the braw wee Scotch lassie at 'em ! |

Doccia recoils from her.

| DOCCIA: | By God ! she frightens me ... |

| MARA-MARA: | *(Accentless)* Let's have some light then, or I'll break my own neck ... |

Lightning, spatter of follow spots on Mara-mara like small searchlights as she advances to hold a bridge. Doccia groans again at the expense.

| DOCCIA: | *(In vain hope)* Have they turned back ? |

| MILORDINO: | *(Now really frightened)* No no ... they haven't. This is serious, they just keep coming. |

| QUAQUEO: | Call Cotrone ! |

| ALL CALL: | "Cotrone ! Cotrone !" |

Cotrone appears casually out of nowhere. ("Now you see him, now you don't !") He is a huge golden bearded man, warm, smiling and expansive in comfortable clothes, shirt of azure silk, black jacket, light baggy trousers. He wears a crumpled fez - illusionist, ventriloquist, souffler, impressionist, magician.

| LA SGRICIA: | *(Nervously angry)* Ah there you are ! Thought perhaps your gout was playing you up ... |

| COTRONE: | You're frightened ... look at you scurrying about frightened and, trying to frighten everyone else ... Duccia ? |

| LA SGRICIA: | ... I thought to myself, his gout has gripped him poor soul, that's what it'll be ... |

DOCCIA:	I know, I know ..
COTRONE:	Aren't you ashamed of yourselves ?
DOCCIA:	I know, I know ...
MILORDINO:	*(Calling down)* More than ten ... !
DOCCIA:	He says a gang of ten ...
QUAQUEO:	No no ... eight, with her ... the woman.

Quaqueo, agitated, grinning his fear.

COTRONE:	Nude ?
QUAQUEO:	Eh ?
COTRONE:	Statuesque ?
QUAQUEO:	Eh ... go on ...
COTRONE:	Without clothes ?
QUAQUEO:	That's what I thought you said. She moves she ... *(Leering through his fear. Might go back for another look.)*
COTRONE:	Come back. Imagine it, if you can.
QUAQUEO:	Oh I can imagine it ...
DOCCIA:	He can imagine it ...
COTRONE:	A dethroned queen.
DOCCIA:	Eh ?
COTRONE:	Stripped of her crown and her throne ...
QUAQUEO:	And her clothes ...

COTRONE: Tossed to the world, her breasts proud, her red hair flowing like blood ... her defrocked bishops, ministers, courtiers harnessed to her coach ... the rooks caw ...*(He caws like a crow.)* the vultures screech ... *(He screeches.)* and the wheels of the coach squeal ...*(He squeals.)* Use a bit of imagination, don't surrender to the mundane, don't go ordinary on me. They can't get us you know ... we regard reason as the excuse of the coward ... do we not ?

MILORDINO: We do, but do they ... huh ?

COTRONE: Do you need that ? What do you care what others believe ... ?

LA SGRICIA: Are they still coming ?

COTRONE: Do you have to be believed in order to believe in yourselves ?

MILORDINO: Nothing stops them, not lightning, not Mara-Mara ... they've seen her, but they still come on !

COTRONE: Of course they do.

Doccia regards Cotrone with sudden suspicion that he knows more than he's saying.

DOCCIA: *(Primly)* In that case I think we can save some electricity, don't you ?

COTRONE: Forget it ... switch off, fetch Mara-Mara from the bridge ... if they haven't been scared into turning back by now they won't be. *(Disingenuously)* Probably in the business, probably pros .. how many ?

Mara-mara coming back.

MILORDINO: Ten ...

MARA-MARA: More than that ...

Lightning and spotlights switched off.

QUAQUEO: Eight ...

Mara-mara trips up on her way back to the others.

MARA-MARA: What have I always said about working lights ... ?

*The Scalognati huddle behind Cotrone,
whispering, still afraid.*

DOCCIA: Who counted them ?

QUAQUEO: I did. Eight ...

COTRONE: He's right ...

MILORDINO: They're here ... alarm !

Cotrone decides.

COTRONE: I know who they are.

DOCCIA: *(Wearily)* Of course you do.

QUAQUEO: 'Course you do, guv.

LA SGRICIA: Gangsters, thugs ... brigands, a band of brigands
... hooligans.

COTRONE: No, not at all ..

He beams a welcome.

*Enter Cromo, Diamante, Battaglia of the
Contessa's company. Cromo's carrot hair - where
he isn't bald - forms two triangles of red, meeting
on top of his head. His voice is that of company
heavy man and manager - sepulchral. He
compliments as he presents his card.*

CROMO: Wonderful effects ! My card ...

COTRONE: Welcome.

> *Cotrone hands the Scalognati the card, it is*
> *squinted at by them all and given back to Cromo*
> *without comment.Diamante gushes.*

DIAMANTE: It was so pretty, and you were so good, it was all
                quite beautiful darlings, loved the hideous green
                fire, wish we could afford it ...

> *Diamante- tall, brittle, in her late thirties with a*
> *shapely body but exaggerated bosom, glitteringly*
> *serious eyes - moves with the arrogant desperate*
> *swagger of a no longer young second female lead.*

QUAQUEO: *(Sickened)* That went down a tonic then didn't it ?

MILORDINO: They enjoyed it ... yes ? Am I right ?

DOCCIA: Total waste. They're legit.

QUAQUEO: I could have scared them more if I'd showed them
                my prick ... or yours ... very ghostly ...

BATTAGLIA: *(Apprehensive)* Ghosts, who said anything about
                ghosts ?

QUAQUEO: I did, ghosts, apparitions, to put the shits up
                nosey. . .

COTRONE: Shut up Quaqueo !

LA SGRICIA: Thank you. Language.

BATTAGLIA: I saw no ghosts . . . did you see ghosts ? I saw
                none . . .

> *Battaglia has the face of a vicious old maid, he*
> *often plays one, come to that he has the face of a*
> *vicious old man as well, he often plays one.*
> *General character utility - sex assumed with wig -*
> *when not on, he's in the prompt corner. Gentle*

pleading eyes belie his appearance.

COTRONE: I knew it! Correct me if I'm wrong ... *(To Cromo)*... you're the Contessa's Company?

CROMO: The same sir !

BATTAGLIA: What's left of it, the remnants ...

DIAMANTE: Say not so, say rather the pillars. *(During this the Count enters.)* Absolutely! We are, thank God, the pillars. *(The Count is a pale young man in a faded and worn but well cut oatmeal suit with a white waistcoat, straw hat on his head, burden of great nobility heavy on his shoulders. He stumbles as he enters and Diamante is instantly and solicitously at his side to support him and receive his vacant smile of condescension and annoyance.)*...this young man is a Count. *(Helping the Count)* Come on, it's all right...

COTRONE: You are welcome, Count.

CROMO: A Count - without a penny left to his name!

DIAMANTE: When will you stop humiliating yourselves, all of you...

COUNT: *(Petulantly)* Nobody may humiliate me !

CROMO: Very well, the man's a Count... *(To Diamante)*... but it might be better if we didn't keep on about it.

DIAMANTE: *(Hissing at Battaglia)* Remnants... speak for yourself, Battaglia.

BATTAGLIA: I did do, love... remnants.

CROMO: *(Of Battaglia)* His modesty is a byword in the profession... you're too modest, old chap.

BATTAGLIA: No, what I am is lightheaded with weariness and hunger.

COTRONE: We can soon do something about that.

LA SGRICIA: No we can't ! The fires are out in the kitchen.

                Mara-mara twirls her parasol, very taken with the Count.

MARA-MARA: Fires? All they need is a ... puff ! Tell us who they are ...

DOCCIA: I wish he would.

COTRONE: I will, I have ... but ... *(To the Count)* ... where is the Contessa herself ?

COUNT: She comes, she's here ... she too is weary ...

BATTAGLIA: She can't stand.

DIAMANTE: Tired, that's all. We're all tired. *(Exasperated)* She might try to make an effort .. occasionally use her own two feet.

                She is bursting with protective instinct towards the Count and against Ilse.

COUNT: *(Shouting in her face)* No she might not ! How dare you !

CROMO: Lumachi is getting his breath back.

BATTAGLIA: His last breath. And she's dead on her feet, own two feet, his last breath, her last legs ... my knees.

CROMO: Can we help ?

COUNT: No, there are enough of them with Lumachi. Where are we ?

CROMO: The nearest hotel ?

BATTAGLIA: Any decent digs, petal ?

CROMO: An eating-house ?

DIAMANTE: I think I'd rather go straight to the theatre ... ?

COTRONE: Please, let me explain ...

COUNT: *(Aloof)* And you are ... ?

> *Shouts and grunts off from Spizzi, Sacerdote,*
> *Lumachi: "One last push, go on, don't let it come*
> *back don't let it come back, take it easy Spizzi,*
> *swing it round ... now ... "*

COTRONE: Ah ... the Contessa !

> *Enter, pulled by Lumachi, pushed by Spizzi and*
> *Sacerdote, on a hand-cart: the Contessa Ilse.*
>
> *Cotrone sweeps off his fez and doesn't put it back*
> *on again for a while.*
>
> *A warning shout from the Count:*

COUNT: Damn you, have care of that cypress branch !

> *The Count galvanised into action to avoid Ilse*
> *being scraped by the cypress tree, he holds it up,*
> *passes it on to Milordino with the command: "...*
> *would you be so kind ?"*

MILORDINO: *(Shocked)* God ! She's pale.

COUNT: No no ...

> *The cart is dragged, pushed to the centre, Lumachi*
> *seeking light and finding it. Lumachi lays down*
> *the burden of the poles and stands back, as do*
> *Spizzi and Sacerdote, their hands out as they back*
> *away presenting the Contessa on the green hay*
> *where she lies. Her dress is simple, worn, of once*

purple blue voile. The sleeves full and long as
if for a taller woman, are pulled back to show
her arms. Her breasts are barely covered. Her
red hair flows like blood, her pallor is that of
death, and there is no sign that she breathes.

MARA-MARA: Dead, stone dead !

SPIZZI: Absolute quiet please !

                    Silence.

                    Then faint notes of music, very faint, a single
                    piano and the slightest movement of the
                    Contessa's's lips. All strain forward to hear.

ILSE: "Listen to me.
                    Listen to what I have to say.
                    Look at what I wear.
                    See the truth of my rags.
                         (Now in full voice)
                    As true as my pain,
                    my sighs.
                    I cry as a mother cries.
                         (She sways suddenly upright)
                    The pain of a mother.
                    The grief of a mother."
                         Laughter from the Contessa'a company,
                         strange, as if scored, indicating scorn and
                         disbelief, ending abruptly, on cue.

ILSE: "How they laugh,
                    you hear them ?
                    the clever people,
                    how they laugh,
                    at my simple tears ... "

COTRONE: Ah ! It's a play ...

                    Milordino and Mara-mara say together:

MILORDINO: It's a play, they're acting, voila !

MARA-MARA: They're giving us a scene ...

DOCCIA: They're legit.

SACERDOTE: Sssssssssh ! Do you mind ? We're trying to perform...

> *Sacerdote is skinny, in a cassock tucked into a belt, legs like matchsticks, gnawed by honesty, juvenile character and utility. He chants, underlines, gestures, interjects throughout but, he is ignored, his is a life of response - the priest.*

ILSE: *(Continuing)* " ... and are unmoved.
More,
furthermore,
in their anger they cry:
Fool ! Fool !
her born son,
impossible !
her born child ... it cannot be !

Hear me,
hear the witness of others,
mothers,
poor mothers like me,
of my village,
of my life
they testify ... "

> *Ilse, hand out waiting for the women to speak, she snaps her finger and thumb impatiently:*

"... the women, the women !"

> *The Count calms her, says soothingly:*

COUNT: They're not here.

ILSE: Why are they not ?

COUNT: They haven't yet arrived.

ILSE: Why have they not ? Where are we ?

MILORDINO: That was so wonderful ... oh. She's so ... oh !

LA SGRICIA: It was so moving ...

DOCCIA: They are so good, that laughter all together ... it
                 sent a shiver down my spine.

LA SGRICIA: I really enjoyed that.

QUAQUEO: See if it's true, see if.

COTRONE: Of course it's true. They're pros my dear ...
                 they're theatricals.

COUNT: *(Objecting)* My wife is hardly ...

ILSE: I'm a theatrical ... I am, you're not, but you come
                 with me ...

COTRONE: Contessa, I hope you don't take offence ...

ILSE: What, at being called a pro ? I like it. It's what I
                 am ... what we are ... it's in my blood, I am born
                 to it. *(To the Count)* You are not, but we've
                 dragged you down with us, have we not ... ?

COUNT: Oh no ... please ... it isn't like that.

ILSE: Yes it is, he falls with me, he's a Count you know,
                 dropped with us onto the cobbles, into the gutter
                 ... we perform anywhere, anywhere ... dragged
                 from his palaces of marble to ... where are we ?
                 Spizzi, where are you ? Lumachi, blow your
                 bloody trumpet. Oh God ... where are we ?
                 Lumachi go through the town, drum up an
                 audience. Sacerdote ? He's a real Count you know
                 - lands, paintings and things ... *(From the protective
                 clutch of Spizzi she pleads, shivering:)* Where are
                 we?

COTRONE: *(Soothingly)* Contessa, you have nothing to fear,
              you are among friends.

CROMO: She isn't at all well. The poor girl's feverish.

QUAQUEO: Who says she's a Countess ?

COUNT: I say she is MY wife !

COTRONE: Be quiet, Quaqueo.

MARA-MARA: That's all very well ...

DOCCIA: They don't any of them look "at all well", to me.

LA SGRICIA: Hhhhhmph ! There's not one I'd leave a child
              with ...

COUNT: We were sent to you.

COTRONE: Indeed you were, signor Conte. I apologise for
              their rudeness, and calling you pros, well,
              theatricals ... I know ...

SPIZZI: You know nothing ! What can you know of this
              lady's Calvary ... her heroic martyrdom ?

              *Spizzi is in love with the Contessa. He is an
              intense eyed young man of just twenty, pale with
              flopping dyed and growing out blond hair, a
              cherub mouth but a rather large nose. Pitifully
              elegant in shabby plus-fours and stockings.
              Juvenile lead.*

ILSE: That's enough, Spizzi ! I forbid it.
              (Pushing herself away from him) You. *(To Cromo,
              hands to his shoulders, glaring at him)* You are the
              one.

CROMO: *(Mystified)* I ?

ILSE: You expected me to sell myself. I heard you say it.

CROMO: What did I say ?

COUNT: Please, don't sink to their level, it is quite horrible
              ... you are above such things surely.

ILSE: Oh but I'm not. Had I not been born an actress I
              might be ... *(She shudders.)* It's too late for all that,
              we are stripped of all that, we must face the
              terrible truth, we must bring everything into the
              open, we're shadows of our former selves, of what
              we once were, and we must face facts. We sleep in
              pigsties !

COUNT: We do not.

ILSE: Last night we slept in a pigsty.

COUNT: *(Patiently)* A bench in a railway station waiting
              room, actually.

CROMO: Third class.

              Ilse ignores them, turns her attention to Cotrone
              and his Scalognati, continues:

ILSE: We sleep in pigsties and third class waiting rooms
              now, all of us together, muttering, mumbling,
              stretching, letting words slip out. *(To Cromo)* It is
              my shame you were the first to believe in me. You.

CROMO: *(Preening)* I think I can claim ...

ILSE: I heard every word ...

CROMO: What ?

ILSE: ... you said. You cannot see, and eyes closed like a
              child you think you cannot be seen or heard. I
              heard you ... as I struggled with spider webs, filthy
              cold wet webs.

COUNT: Heavens, Ilse ... hardly that.

ILSE: Cold drifts of darkness then, fluttering on my face, breathing wraiths then ... icy breath on my hot brow, cheeks, slithering down my neck ... I heard you and I laughed. Like this, I laughed: "hehee hehee" then for fear of hysteria I clenched tight my jaws, so that I would not yelp like a thrashed bitch yelps ... "Ehee, ehee ... ehee ehee ehee ..." I went, "Ehee, ehee ... ehee ehee ehee ..." Did you not hear it ? YOU ?

CROMO: I did not ...

ILSE: Oh yes ... you did ... you thought it was a chuckle of complicity, the laughter of someone snuggle agreeing with you, in the dark ...

CROMO: I remember none of this !

ILSE: I remember all of this !

SPIZZI: What dared he say ?

ILSE: What does he always say ? Good contracts, good clothes, good stones, good furs, good parts, good notices, first class travel, accommodation and acclamation, have all got to be paid for he says, he always says. How much better he said, would it be he said did I not have to suffer my Calvary and you also, all of you, not be forced to suffer it with me, when all-was-needed-was ... ?

CROMO: *(Uncomfortably)* Yes. I did say that.

ILSE: Yes.

CROMO: I am not alone. And those of us who don't say it, think it ... him too.

COUNT: Me ?

CROMO: You.

COUNT: What ?

ILSE: You think I should have given myself ... without
                 another thought. *(Her hands around the Count's
                 head, her face close, looking into his eyes, her fingers
                 on his forehead)* All was needed was just one little
                 fuck ... *(To Cromo)*... yes ?

CROMO: If you choose to put it that way. At least now we
                 would not be in danger of starving.

ILSE: Without another thought !
                 And you my noble husband would now have two
                 little horns on your noble forehead for all to see
                 and whisper ... just here, and here ....

                      *Ilse with fingers up like horns at her husband's
                      head and about to affix them, instead turns on
                      Cromo and with an "Aaaagh !" of disgust and the
                      back of a hand and wrist hits him hard across his
                      face; a stinging blow which astonishes him as
                      much as it hurts him. She then flings herself to the
                      ground in violent convulsions of laughter and
                      tears.
                      For a moment All are stunned by the action.*

                      *Then, as Cotrone, the Count and Diamante go to
                      help Ilse to her feet, Quaqueo, Doccia, Mara-mara
                      and Milordino applaud; Sacerdote, Lumachi,
                      Battaglia and La Sgricia huddle and agonise; and
                      Cromo and Spizzi square up to each other.*

                      Count, Cotrone, Diamante and Ilse say together:

COUNT: Oh my God, I fear for her sanity, Ilse ... Ilse ..

COTRONE: Contessa, let me help you ... please, let me help
                 you up. Why don't we try to get her over here ...
                 Contessa please take my ..

DIAMANTE: You must try to pull yourself together Ilse, for the
                 sake of your dear husband if nothing ....

ILSE: NO ! Let me go, leave me alone, let me say it ...

Quaqueo, Doccia, Mara-mara amd Milordino say together:

QUAQUEO: She's very good, she got straight to the point ... you have to pay for everything, no such thing as a free ...*(Going coy)*... anything ...

DOCCIA: A quite remarkable performance, we shall not see the like very often ...

MARA-MARA: He doesn't know how to ride a blow but perhaps she didn't fake it ...

MILORDINO: Who ...

Battaglia, Lumachi, La Sgricia, Sacerdote speak together.

Lumachi, stolid pipe smoking practical north countryman and simpleton, stage carpenter, manager, flyposter.

BATTAGLIA: There are things should never be said dears, you end up diggin' your own grave ... I do.

LUMACHI: It's beyond me, such a little thing, such violence over nothing, nothing at all ...

MILORDINO: Who ...

LA SGRICIA: *(Crossing herself)* Heavenly Father protect me, I am set down in Bedlam, it's a jungle, it's a battlefield ... They're Turks !

SACERDOTE: I have to say it, she's not wrong when she says what she says ...

MILORDINO: Who ...

Spizzi and Cromo speaking together:

CROMO: Don't you lay your hands on me young man, get out of my way, I've just about had enough of you, and of her and of the whole silly ...

SPIZZI: You shit, you absolute shit Cromo, you absolute cowardly shit ... you are the sort of man would sell his wife ...

ILSE: ... I want everybody to hear what I have to say.

MILORDINO: ... on earth let them out of the bin ... eh?

            Sacerdote's chant is heard:

SACERDOTE: ... we have all said it !

CROMO: As a matter of fact WE don't matter, I refer to the young man who killed himself.

ILSE: Have you ALL said it ?

SPIZZI: Certainly not.

            Sacerdote mutters throughout as punctuation to their protestations:

SACERDOTE: Did ...

DIAMANTE: I didn't utter a word.

SACERDOTE: Did do ...

BATTAGLIA: Well I didn't, you know me.

SACERDOTE: Did ...

ILSE: *(To the Count)* You thought it though ?

SACERDOTE: Yes ...

COUNT: Me ? ... I don't think we should discuss this in front of strangers, Ilse.

SACERDOTE: No.

COTRONE: Signor Conte, please don't give us a thought ...

ILSE: Oh but we must give it a thought. *(Smiling charmingly)* Forgive me but we must.

COTRONE: As if we're not here, Contessa.
              We're on holiday, open hearted, responsive,
              amiable loafers ...

ILSE: Countess ? I'm an actress.
              There are some need reminding that this is an
              honourable calling.

CROMO: Some of us try not to make such a big thing of it. I
              have always been an actor. I have been loyal to the
              company and I have stayed no matter what. I seem
              to remember there was a time you turned your
              back on the profession.

COUNT: That is untrue ! It was I insisted she leave the
              stage.

CROMO: And who is to say you were wrong old chap ? Pity
              it didn't stay that way, you a Count and me of
              none, I might have kept my mouth shut, might
              have not regarded myself as a chum, free to speak
              his mind, all chums together .. *(To Ilse)* You had
              married your Count ... *(Aside to the others)* ... very
              rich. *(To Ilse again)*... you weren't any more an
              actress intent on keeping her reputation when all
              about were losing theirs and indeed thinking
              nothing of it.

              And a good actress, brilliant and with integrity I
              know you were, we all know you were ...
              reputation unsullied ... as it were.

ILSE: Exactly ! Always !

CROMO: Perhaps a little too rigorously unsullied,
sweetheart. And once you achieved Countess! Eh?
Countesses are expected to be ... generous, and on
the whole they are ... at it like knives. *(Ilse holding
herself very still - Cromo takes a good breath and:)*
Nobody would have thought the worse of you and
the poor wretch wouldn't have killed himself and
you me all of us not forgetting the Count poor
chap wouldn't be in the shit we are undoubtedly
in today ... tonight ! *(A pause - a sigh and to the
Count a shrug:)* What are friends for ? Chum.

SACERDOTE: Oh dear.

*From Ilse, rigid and erect as if bound with iron
there comes the strange laugh.*

ILSE: Ehee .... ehee ehee ehee ehee ehee ehee ehee
...*(Fingers up she makes the horns of a cuckold and
rasps:)*   On a husband they are the horns of a
cuckold, on a butterfly they are called antennae ...

The Count controls himself but tells Cromo icily:

COUNT: You have gone too far. You are no longer welcome
amongst us. Be so kind as to go ! At once !

CROMO: Are you paying me off ? What with ?

ILSE: *(Quickly to her husband)* He's right. What with ?
(To Cotrone) That's the way it is, we are not taking
enough to pay them to play.

SPIZZI: *(Confused, indignant)* I don't think so ... that's not
so.

ILSE: It is not so about you. It is so regarding him.
CROMO: Bloody well isn't ! Remuneration ? I'd have gone
before today if it was about pay, as others have ...
I'm still here because there are more important
things than money, there's you ... and there's ...

Ilse screams at him desperation:

ILSE:	What do you expect me to do ?

CROMO: Too late now darling, all gone, sluiced ... you
should have asked me before that sad suicide did
for himself and entered our souls like a malignant
growth ... look at us; whipped from pillar to post,
a pack of half starved whining strays. You, look at
you; imperious, disdainful, erect with integrity but,
your wings are draggled, droop. Your beak is up
but, tied with a loop of twine like bunches of
thrushes for sale in the market...

QUAQUEO: Who killed himself ?

La Sgricia tugs on the skirt of Ilse's dress, asks:

LA SGRICIA: Was it one of them ?

Ilse beams kindly on La Sgricia:

ILSE: No no you dear sweet kind old soul, no he was a
man head and shoulders above them, he was a
poet.

COTRONE: Oh surely not ... !

SPIZZI: If I may enlighten you; the Countess refers to the
author of our play "The Tale of the Changeling
Prince", which we have toured for the past two
years ...

SACERDOTE: That's right ...

COTRONE: I know.

SPIZZI: Dare you say he was no poet ?

COTRONE: I doubt he killed himself for it.

CROMO: He killed himself for love of her ! *(Pointing wearily)*
Disastrously poetic.

COTRONE: Because the Contessa, faithful to her vows rejected his love - good.
Please don't blame poetry.
On the whole, poets tend to write poems, not kill themselves - grand.

ILSE: He ... *(Accusing Cromo)* ... says I should have let the young poet ... love me, now a countess ... as if a title excuses unfaithfulness ...

COUNT: When only the heart does that.

ILSE: Yes. Does it ?

CROMO: She loved him.

SACERDOTE: She did ...

ILSE: Yes. Did I ?

CROMO: I should bloody well hope so, not much point to it all otherwise, about the only thing can be said in your favour, the rest is without merit; actually, one should never fail to respond to the heart's promptings ... much better in the long run. For instance your husband would be a happier and richer man.

COUNT: Have you quite finished telling the world ?

CROMO: I didn't start it.

COUNT: You did.

QUAQUEO: And got slapped for it.

> *Laughter. Ilse reaches out to Cromo, full of sympathy, kisses her palm and caresses his cheek.*

ILSE: Let me kiss it better. Is it gone ? You're not the enemy my dear, much as you try to be.

CROMO: *(Responding)* But I don't.

ILSE: With your stiletto, you do darling, and for all to see ...

CROMO: I stab you ?

ILSE: What else ? *(To Cotrone)* It's the sort of thing happens in the gutter. *(To the Count)* If only you could be allowed a shred of dignity, poor love. Cheer up, soon be over ... I feel the end is quite close.

COUNT: Please, you must not talk like that. *(To Cotrone)* All she needs is a rest.

ILSE: Rest ? Sleep is torn from my eyes ! What are you hoping to hide ? Don't. An innocent may bare his soul ... as a child may step out of clothes. *(She starts.)* Good Lord, I do believe we're in the country ... and it's dark, and there are people ... yes. *(To her husband)* I loved him and I made his death for him, I gave him nothing else ... just that, this dead poet with us still. *(To Cotrone)* I have lived in a dream, as if perpetually crossing an ocean, I am as if alive after witnessing my death ... in those days I was a person called Ilse Paulsen.

COTRONE: I know, Contessa ...

ILSE: I had a good name in the theatre.

COUNT: Spotless.

CROMO: Did I say it wasn't ? She was on another plane, mind you she has always been quite excitable. Before she married him she was going to become a nun, picture it if you can.

SPIZZI: And you dare to expect her to change once she became a Countess !

CROMO: I thought I had explained that.

SACERDOTE: He did.

ILSE: I have taken on a sacred duty. *(She addresses
                 Cotrone.)* A friend of my husband, a Poet came: in
                 his hands an unfinished play he wished for me
                 without hope I would consider it, for he knew I
                 had abandoned the stage for my husband; might
                 he read it me ?

                 And oh, it was going to be beautiful ...*(To Cromo)*
                 ... yes, it excited me. *(To Cotrone again)* Though I
                 knew what he was doing - a woman becomes
                 aware quickly - he wanted his play on and he
                 wanted me to do it.

                 Poets know their words are their means to their
                 ends.

                 He hoped to entice me back to my former life with
                 his alluring piece not for the sake of the work but
                 for himself, he wanted me ... what to do ? Did I
                 say no he wouldn't finish it and that would be
                 grave, did I say yes such is the inconstancy of
                 poets he might abandon it, his baser desire
                 achieved ... ... me.

                 I nourished him in his hopes, I blew gently on the
                 coals and when the forge roared I drew back,
                 watched the exquisite shaping. Aware too late,
                 that as the precious metal cooled into its beautiful
                 glittering contortion so too did I ... melt.
                 (Indicating Cromo) That man is right. My
                 constancy during the forging was annealed by the
                 Poet's death. I denied him life, I give life to his
                 work.

                 With the consent of my husband I returned to my
                 former existence ... for a limited season only. This
                 play alone !

CROMO: Ordination and martyrdom ! The High Priestess of
                 Art. And he, the noble Count was never jealous, at

no time, not ever.

COUNT: I find no cause.

SACERDOTE: That's right ...

CROMO: Consider this cause; to her He is not dead, she wills He should live, she lives for Him so completely she wastes, will die in rags and take us with her so that He, the author of our play and our fate may live ! Makes you want to puke.

DIAMANTE: You're the one jealous of him.

CROMO: Bravo ! The nail on the head.

DIAMANTE: You're all in love with her !

SACERDOTE: Yes ...

CROMO: No. It's annoyance and compassion.

ILSE: His invective exalts me !

SPIZZI: He has that ability !

BATTAGLIA: I hate this, all this spiritual stuff ... you don't know where you are !

LUMACHI: *(Folding his arms)* Another fine mess we've got ourselves into ..

ILSE: Oh, it will lead to my death. I accept the chalice. Had I known the pain it would cause me ... his pain, in his work ... found by me ...

COTRONE: Your poet's play, pearls before swine, has been your ruin ... you don't have to tell me, you really don't.

BATTAGLIA: From the first performance on.

COTRONE: They wouldn't have it ?

SACERDOTE: Died a death.

CROMO: When they start coming AT you ...

COTRONE: *(Laughing ruefully)* I know, I know ...

ILSE: Do you find it funny ?

COTRONE: Oh no Contessa, I understand too well that the
                work of a poet ...

DIAMANTE: Meant bugger all. Even the sets went for nothing.
                Shits.

BATTAGLIA: *(A great sigh)* Beautifully lit too.

CROMO: A first-class production, quite spectacular and
                what a cast, forty two of us including walk-ons...!

COTRONE: Of which just you few are left ?

CROMO: *(Indicating his shabbiness)* Rags my dear. " The
                work of a Poet"

COUNT: *(Bitterly)* You had a hand in it too.

CROMO: *(Indicating the Count)* He's lost everything he had.

COUNT: I don't regret it. I made my choice.

ILSE: Well said. Worthy of you !

COUNT: I mean it. I don't get excited over nothing. I
                believe in the play ...

COTRONE: When I talk of "the work of a poet" I intend no
                disrespect signor Conte, I reserve my contempt for
                those who reject you.

COUNT: Yes. Very well. Those who disparage the play
                disparage my wife and render as nothing her
                efforts and her genius. I have lost a fortune and I

have lost nothing if she is happy and fulfilled
in the beauty and the greatness of the work
she undertakes ... yes ... well ... if all this is for
... if we suffer abuse for ... you know what I
mean, if we put up with ridicule and ...
You see ... it's no good, I can't go on ...

> *The Count can say no more, he is overcome
> with emotion.*

SACERDOTE: Oh ...

COTRONE: There there, I understand ... I hate them all ...
the general public... that's why I live here. See
here, the proof ! *(He claps the fez onto his
head.)* I was once a Christian, I am now a
Turk !

LA SGRICIA: That's enough of that ...*(Crossing herself)*...
there's no need to drag religion into it.

SACERDOTE: Oh dear ...

COTRONE: This is no concern of the Prophet peace be on
him, I wear a fez only because the poetry of
Christianity has failed lamentably . . . But,
signor Conte has the reception of your play
been wholly hostile ?

COUNT: Oh no, some people like it very much ... there
are one or two kind people ...

SPIZZI: Who think it's wonderful ...

ILSE: But not a lot !

COUNT: ... who've given it a rave.

CROMO: *(Soberly)* All the number one dates are denied
us since Berlin banned it. We can only get the
fleapits and now they say no because we're
down to four m's and two f's - no frocks,
props.

COUNT: That is not true ! You have all you need.

SACERDOTE: Well ...

BATTAGLIA: The costumes are in the cart ...

LUMACHI: Under the hay.

SPIZZI: And anyway we don't need them.

CROMO: What about the set ?

COUNT: We can do without.

BATTAGLIA: Though I rarely have more than a cough and a spit
              I play as cast, man or woman.

CROMO: So we've noticed.

BATTAGLIA: Oh isn't she sharp !

SACERDOTE: In short, we do the lot ... I do my best, I ...

DIAMANTE: We don't cut a line, you get the lot - if we can't
              wing it we read it.

SPIZZI: It's SO good that nobody cares about actors or
              props.

SACERDOTE: Oh yes ...

COUNT: *(To Cotrone)* They're talking rubbish, we've got
              everything we need ... we really should stop having
              such a low opinion of ourselves. I think we're jolly
              good !

COTRONE: I do like your spirit ! But you don't have to tell me
              it's a very good production of a very beautiful play.
              You were sent to me by a dear friend of mine - I
              only wish he'd been able to stop you coming all
              this way.

COUNT:	Why ?
SPIZZI:	Is there nothing here ?
CROMO:	I knew it !
SACERDOTE:	Oh oh ...
LUMACHI:	What did I say ? Up a blooming mountain !
COTRONE:	Don't worry, we'll think of something.
DIAMANTE:	Where ?
COTRONE:	I hope you haven't left anything in the town ...
SACERDOTE:	*(He has)* Oh ...
COUNT:	Isn't there a theatre ?
COTRONE:	Full of mice. It's kept locked. Even if it wasn't nobody would go.
QUAQUEO:	There are plans to redevelop it.
COTRONE:	That's right ... into a stadium, fights and things ...
MARA-MARA:	No, it's going to be a cinema.
COTRONE:	That's right, chases and things.
COUNT:	Where shall we go ? There isn't an audience here.
DIAMANTE:	What a dump !
SPIZZI:	We came to you ...
COTRONE:	And we are here, and at your service ... don't let it worry you, we can find room .. you must be exhausted ... please go in, make yourselves comfortable.
BATTAGLIA:	Any chance of any grub ?

COTRONE: You'll have to make do as we do.

BATTAGLIA: Eh ? Do ... ?

DOCCIA: Without ... then you don't need anything.

BATTAGLIA: Eh ?

QUAQUEO: *(To Doccia)* Don't ... they might not stay.

BATTAGLIA: We need everything.

COTRONE: Go in, go in.

BATTAGLIA: How can you manage with nothing ?

COTRONE: Contessa ?

        *Ilse alone. She stares at Cotrone and nods
        vacantly.*

COUNT: She'll come in later.

DIAMANTE: Do you want to go in ?

SACERDOTE: Oh ...

CROMO: Who wants to stay out in the damp all night ? Do
                you ?

SACERDOTE: ... no.

BATTAGLIA: Even so ... you must eat ?

COTRONE: Yes yes, see what you can do Mara-Mara ...

MARA-MARA: Come on in ... all it needs is a little puff ...

LUMACHI: I'm not going down that mountain again ...

        He has no tobacco for his pipe, fumbles.

QUAQUEO: Why not, you've got a cart.

LUMACHI: Yes but I pull it, Titch.

MILORDINO: The less you eat, the better you sleep.

BATTAGLIA: To start with petal, then the yearning eats into
                your sleep and your gut ...

COTRONE: Leave the cart, it'll be all right. Duccio, find
                beds...

SPIZZI: The Countess will need a suite.

CROMO: We all need rooms.

MILORDINO: We've got suites, we've got rooms.

LA SGRICIA: Nobody gets my room !

COTRONE: Nobody wants your room, it's got the organ in it.

QUAQUEO: It's where we say our prayers, come on, I'll give
                you a tune ... *(Pushing them into the villa)*
                "Seated one day at my organ I got a big surprise! "

LA SGRICIA: Don't you dare you little devil !

                *Exit all except Ilse, Cotrone and the Count, into
                the villa.*
                *Cotrone whistles: "In a Monastery Garden"
                beautifully, complete with bird noises while the
                light changes.*

                        END OF ACT ONE

ACT TWO

Scene: villa called "La Scalogna". Italy. 1937. Night.

Cotrone stops whistling and there is silence. Light has changed from dusk to cloud-obscured moon. The first shaft of moonlight illumines Ilse.

ILSE: Five tomcats surround one queen
                   waiting and watching her
                   consumed with lust for her,
                   they mew and quiver and
                   sheath and unsheathe their claws,
                   their eyes never leave her but
                   should one move, all move ...

COTRONE: *(Assures her)* There is a room with a key for the
                   Countess ...

COUNT: *(To Cotrone)* Shhhhh ...

COTRONE: *(Hushed)* Ah ... is she doing the play ? Saying her
                   lines ?

COUNT: Not her lines .. *(Then in another voice to Ilse)*
                   "Oh yes, blame it on the cat ..."

ILSE: "Is it queen cats leap
                   smother,
                   on the heads
                   of babies
                   smother,
                   scratch, squabble, bite
                   on the heads of babies
                   in their cots at night ?
                   Look at this!
                   Look at this ! "

COUNT: "Look at what ?"

ILSE: "This plait of hair,
                   done by fingers,
                   in the dark,

tangled, matted where
the little head has lain.
(Then changing her character and her voice, and as if
cradling a child)
No, my golden boy !"

Ilse changes her character again, and the Count
joins her in some of the sad song, music looping in
and around the words, he softer than her,
prompting and encouraging, sometimes simply
mouthing, in the end silent as Ilse's voice swells.

ILSE: "See, woe, let
not
scissors near,
not comb nor
steel shear,
one cut and
see his golden
head
see, the child is
dead ... "

COUNT: "Woe ... see
not comb
not steel
dead
his golden
head
see
woe
see, the child is
dead ... "

COTRONE: The Countess has an enchanting voice.

COUNT: Yes.

COTRONE: She'll feel better inside.

COUNT: Ilse ... ?

COTRONE: Of the necessities of life we have none ... much,

but of everything else we have more than we need,
all I have to do is ask ... what about dawn ? *(He
cups his hands and calls:)* Would you be so kind ... ?
(Pink dawn illuminates the wall of the villa.) There !

> *Ilse claps her hands once, twice, in little girl
> delight.*

ILSE: Oh that's lovely !

COTRONE: Isn't it ?

COUNT: How did you do it ?

COTRONE: I'm a magician. It's a modest living ... look ! *(He
             snaps his fingers and the moonlight is back.)* If night's
             blackness is created for anything it's for fireflies.
             There ... there ... and there. *(He points with his
             finger and where he points each time there is a glow of
             green activity, fleeting glimpses of phantom fireflies far
             away up the mountainside. They glow and fade.)*
             They call me the Great Cotrone !

ILSE: Heavens, how ..?

COUNT: What on earth !?

COTRONE: Fireflies. Mine. Magical. We sit on the edges of
             life in this place and at a magician's command the
             edges blur and things which can't be seen become
             light, shadows, film - perfectly natural
             phenomenon, happens all the time in dreams. I
             can do it for those of us awake as well.
             Dreams, music, prayer, love, all that is infinite.

             > *Chatter and organ music from inside the villa, a
             > screech, and enter La Sgricia excessively irritated.*

LA SGRICIA: This won't do, you've got to be told ... HE won't
             want to come if this goes on. I warn you ! *(She
             glares.)* And then where would we be ?

COTRONE: He'll come, Sgricia ...

Another burst of organ and excited talk from in the villa.

LA SGRICIA: Not if they keep that up! *(She strains to hear.)* What are they saying ? Devils !

COTRONE: Idle chatter, words can't harm you. *(Arm out)* Come here, let me present you to the Contessa. *(To Ilse, introducing)* La Sgricia. Who says prayers for us all, quite a lot. She is La Sgricia of the Angel and His Hundred. She joined us when the Church rejected her miracle.

ILSE: What Hundred ?

COTRONE: A battle of a hundred souls in Purgatory who ride on holy work. Nightly at eleven thirty.

ILSE: Oh yes ? And the miracle ?

COTRONE: Tell her ... tell the Contessa about your miracle, Sgricia.

LA SGRICIA: I don't like to, she won't believe me ... you won't believe me mum.

ILSE: But I will, I will believe you.

COTRONE: Believe me, none will believe you more readily than the Contessa. *(He tries to persuade.)* Tell her. *(Gives up.)* What happened was that she was on her way to see one of her sisters who lived in the next village ..

A Voice heard, clear, flat and from somewhere in the air above:

VOICE: A shitpit of iniquity, like a lot of others on this savage island.

COTRONE: *(Hastily reassuring)* It's all right ...

The Voice again, this time from the cypress behind Ilse and startling her with its proximity:

VOICE: They kill people like flies.

ILSE: Who is that ?

COUNT: Where does it come from ?

COTRONE: Please Contessa, it's all right, the voices form in the air.

LA SGRICIA: It's the dead, the murdered ...

She says with great and ghoulish relish. Then she notices that Cotrone is shaking his head and assuring the Count and Ilse behind his hand:

COTRONE: No no ...

La Sgricia attacks him angrily:

LA SGRICIA: No ? What do you mean, no ? It's the Child !

Cotrone quickly agrees, humouring La Sgricia, but another wink at the Count.

COTRONE: It is, it is ... the Child. *(Then to Ilse he continues:)* There is the story of a little boy on his way somewhere given a lift by someone and murdered for the few pennies in his pocket. The murderer tossed the boy's corpse into a ditch from his cart and went on his way under the stars ...

LA SGRICIA: Under the eyes of God, that's what he went on his way under, so much so that he went straight to the nearest police station and opened his mouth, the pennies clutched in his bloody hands and said ... *(Shivering and crossing herself)* WITH THE VOICE OF THE POOR SLAUGHTERED CHILD: "I did it !" That's what God can do.

COTRONE: Of course he can, which is why you should never

be afraid of the dark if you have the faith of
Sgricia.

LA SGRICIA: It wasn't supposed to be dark. If he hadn't
brought the donkey round when he did I'd have
gone in the morning ...

COTRONE: This was a farming fellow wanted to marry her
once ...

LA SGRICIA: *(Another glare)* And that's got nothing to do with it
... ! When I got on the donkey I looked up and I
knew it wasn't morning but when you're a poor
old woman what can you do ? He was giving me
the lend of his donkey ... and if he thought it was
morning ... ? So I crossed myself, naturally, and
set off ...

COTRONE: Under God's eyes.

LA SGRICIA: That's right, under the stars, under the moon ...
that's why he thought it was morning, the moon ...
such shadows, deep shadows ... awful shadows
and from the road the land slipped away ... and so
quiet, even the donkey's hooves muffled by the
dust, a long white road stretching for ever and the
moon showing it stretching for ever and me with
my shawl pulled down over my head for them
shadows ... I must have nodded off but I woke, in
the middle of soldiers.

COTRONE: Yes ... listen, listen ...

LA SGRICIA: I felt much better thank you very much, troopers
on big horses on each side of me, led by a Captain
on a white horse, lovely animal. Thank God I
thought, I'm safe now, shadows or no ... thank
you very much God I said but, no sound, not a
wink or a laugh from these young chaps none of
them more than twenty and I must have been a
strange sight - an old woman on a donkey in the
middle of the night. And no dust from their horses

hooves, I made dust, they didn't, or sound ... why?
Yes. All the way to the village. At Favara they halt,
stand the way they do, soldiers, daybreak shining
through them, the Captain on his great white
stallion, shoulders, legs, waiting for me on my
little donkey, moon gone, flags flapping without a
sound. *(She booms.)* "Sgricia ! I am the Hangel of
the Century of God and these what have excorted
you through the shadows of the moon and night is
souls in Purgatory and as soon as you enter the
village make your peace with God and for you will
DIE before noon !" Yes. That's right.

COTRONE: Here comes the best bit ...*(Cotrone prompts.)*
               When her sister saw her, pale, shuddering, er ...
               moonstruck ... !

LA SGRICIA: "What's up ?" she said."Get me a priest" I said.
               "What's wrong ?" she said."I'm going to die before
               twelve o-clock" I said ...*(She opens her arms.)* ...
               (Looking into Ilse's eyes she asks) Do you think
               you're alive ?

                    *La Sgricia has a finger up in front of Ilse, she
                    slowly wags it. The Voice startles Ilse again it is
                    so close, from the cypress.*

VOICE: Don't believe it !

                    *Exit La Sgricia into the villa with a nod and a
                    smile at Ilse expressing great satisfaction and:
                    "You hear that ? What did I tell you ?".*

ILSE: She thinks she's dead ?

COTRONE: She thinks she's in another world Contessa - with
               the rest of us.

ILSE: *(Uneasy)* What are the voices ?

COTRONE: Do they worry you ?

COUNT: Do you do them ?

COTRONE: They might help you accept another truth -
            removed from your own truth though every bit as
            fleeting and changeable - in which ... *(To Ilse)* ...
            an old lady sees an Angel and a hundred horsemen
            from Purgatory. Don't try to apply reason. It's the
            way we live. We've got nothing but a lot of time,
            incomprehensible wealth, and an ebullience of
            rash fancy. Nothing exists unless we can find a
            place in our imagination for it and, we don't do
            anything much but imagine, laze about ... placidly
            conceive mythological atrocities - angels are two-a-
            penny. We breathe vaporous thoughts, the air
            hangs with flavours, air-drawn daggers, voices,
            laughter, ideas we give birth to, comprehend, but
            don't completely understand. Every shadow
            squirms. We detest dull and silent shadows and fill
            them with motes of colour lodged from our last
            look at the sun ...*(He listens.)* We don't think up
            the shapes, our eyes do it for us ...*(He listens
            again.)* Here she comes.*(He shouts.)* Maddalena !
            (Then points) There, on a bridge.

            *A spurt of flame and Maria Maddalena appears,
            young, red hair, red labouring clothes, she is lit by
            the red light of the lantern she carries.*

ILSE: Who is that ?

COTRONE: It's the Girl in Red. Don't be scared, she's not an
            apparition, far from it, she's all too successfully
            flesh and blood. Come here Maddalena ... there's
            a good girl.*(Maddalena approaches, smiling.)* Sad
            smiling innocent, a bit simple, she can feel but she
            can't say so. All alone, none to care she wanders
            hoiking up her skirts to offer men herself, giving
            herself, leaving her brats where they drop on the
            grass a smile of pleasure given and taken
            constantly on her lips and in her eyes ...She comes
            - go on in Maddalena - almost every night to
            shelter ... go in ...*(Maddalena nods several times.)*
            She hasn't the faintest idea - go on in - what it is
            that happens to her. There's a good girl.

Exit Maria Maddalena into the villa, sad eyes,
sweet smile, gone.

ILSE: **Which** family has the villa ?

COTRONE: Nobody but us. Perhaps the spirits.

COUNT: Spirits ?

ILSE: Of what ?

COTRONE: They scared off the family.

ILSE: I doubt you believe in ghosts.

COTRONE: We create them.

ILSE: Do you though ... ?

COTRONE: That's saucy coming from you, an actress. What
             else do you do but give form to phantasms ? We
             reverse the process, make phantoms of our bodies,
             just as real as yours on the stage ...Come now, you
             are a shadow of your former self Contessa ...
             would you say ? You did say.

ILSE: I am, and less ... and less !

COTRONE: There ! A shadow of your former self. But
             something else is still there, alive inside you. The
             spirit of the young man who killed himself for you,
             isn't he within you, alive, more than a shadow ?

ILSE: Within me ... oh yes.

COTRONE: *(Pointing at the villa)* Like to see him?

ILSE: *(In horror)* No !

COTRONE: Abracadabra !

             Light on the pale face of a young man standing in

a doorway dressed in evening dress, cloak, top-hat,
the cloak held elegantly, a flashlight hidden in the
cloak to light the face of Spizzi who impersonates
the dead poet. Ilse shrieks and collapses, her face in
her hands. Spizzi runs to her in consternation.

SPIZZI: Ilse it's a joke ...

COUNT: Spizzi ! Ilse it's a joke ...

SPIZZI: It's me ... my God !

COUNT: It's Spizzi ...

COTRONE: He's emerged ...

COUNT: What are you talking about ?

COTRONE: The truth ! He's let it come out.

SPIZZI: We're having a laugh ...

COTRONE: If you want the truth, invent it ! Mind you, every
            time I do I'm accused of lying ... but, you say you
            were joking ... ? *(To Spizzi)* Then what made you
            choose what you chose ? And here's more proof.
            (More faces lit by torches, Diamante, Cromo,
            Battaglia, Lumachi. To Diamante, Cotrone says:)
            You wear the tiara of a Contessa. *(Taking*
            Diamante by the hand, Cotrone presents her asking
            the Count, puzzled:) Were you ever at Court ?

COUNT: No, never, why ?

COTRONE: She's dressed as a Lady of the Bedchamber .. *(To*
            Battaglia)... like a tortoise in its shell you found
            your home in the skirts of a vicious old woman ...
            (To Lumachi in donkey skin and head)... you could
            think of nothing but the donkey you want to pull
            the cart ... you ...*(To Cromo dressed as a very rich*
            oriental, white tuxedo, cummerbund, jewel in
            turban)... Pasha, are quite splendid, you know
            what it's all about ... la dolce vita ! And a kind

heart.

COUNT: What on earth is going on ?

CROMO: My dear they have a vast wardrobe.

LUMACHI: You should see. Everything, better than a costumier ...

COTRONE: You each took what you wanted, the mask you wanted to wear ...

SPIZZI: It was just a joke ...

COTRONE: *(Irritably)* You think what you are wearing is a joke !

ILSE: It isn't a joke. They were told what to wear.

COUNT: By whom ?

ILSE: The magician ... you.

COTRONE: Oh no, Contessa ...

ILSE: I know what you do. You say you invent the truth?

COTRONE: Oh yes, I do that, I've always done that, I can't help doing that, I persuade truth from people, from deep down in them, some of the nastiest stuff is very deep down, it can be painful. I did invent rather a lot once and had to exit left pursued by Scandals. What we do here is tone them down a bit, chuck them into the wind as it were, all colours, all shapes, blown, dispersed, sharp visions that spray into evanescence, passing shadows, even that which is real we kick into clouds, mists, gusts of soul, into night and dreams.

CROMO: *(Prosaically)* Something in the nature of son et lumière ? Fireworks ?

COTRONE: Without the bangs. A lot of silent fiery

enchantment, keeps the general public at bay -
usually the green tongue is enough - that's how we
manage to stay here without anybody asking
questions, the odd ghost.

CROMO: How do you live ?

COTRONE: Like this, everything and nothing.

DOCCIA: *(Earnestly)* You can only have everything if you've
got nothing ...

CROMO: Is that a fact ? *(To the Count)* Hear that do you ?
That means we've got everything ... you could've
fooled me ...

COTRONE: Ah, that's because you still want something.

MARA-MARA: *(Primly)* One may sleep without a mattress.

CROMO: Excruciatingly.

MARA-MARA: Nevertheless, one may.

DOCCIA: Exhausted ... you sleep.

COTRONE: Bread tastes much better when you're hungry than
when it sits at the side of your plate. Quaqueo will
illustrate ...

> *Quaqueo does, hand revolving on stomach, knees
> moving, tongue licking.*

DOCCIA: If you're without a roof you're a tenant of the
world, you sink down into the grass under the
silent stars and you are nothing as well as being
everything ... sort of thing ...

BATTAGLIA: *(Wearily)* Oh yes love ?

COTRONE: Such is the philosophy of beggars Contessa, some
of them, the noble ones who have been able to
reach that exquisite condition in which beggary

becomes a privilege. You don't find mediocrity in beggars, only among the respectable and the parsimonious. Doccia looks after the money, his money, he has saved a little here and a little there throughout his life and putting it all together wanted for a charity and found us. He pays. Green fire, flash powder, that sort of thing ... and the schmutter of course.

DOCCIA: *(Uneasily)* We ought to have a talk ...

COTRONE: *(With delight)* He's so fucking mean !

               Roars of laughter and agreement from the Scalognati:

SCALOGNATI: It's true ! He is ! Tightarse !

COTRONE: He's trying to make it last longer. Well here's a secret at once no more. Your world once held me and I could have been something as they say, gone to the top, had I not retired, resigned, left decorum, honour, dignity, virtue hanging on pegs ... once you've jerked that lot off if you've still got a soul it does feel very lively and large, like air with sunshine and clouds open to lightning strikes, thunder bolts, winds light, slight or monstrous, the superfluous stuff of marvels whirling you into mystery, fabulous longinquity. Look down there at sad Earth where some think they live their own lives and don't come near. The body you see is not what there is it's only the soul can speak of what there is and, who knows from where the soul gets its words ? We're appearances through appearances to appearances with funny names like Cotrone, like Doccia ... like Quaqueo ... a body is a corpse benighted, and stone. I wouldn't like to be the man who thinks he's there in his body with his name, would rather be the very first ghost comes into my head, to moan. We've inherited some, like the braw wee Scots lassie with the umbrella. *(Mara-mara)* How she got here we'll never know but the punters expect it. And there's an occasional guest appearance of the blue nosed dwarf. *(Quaqueo takes a bow.)* Specialities of the house ... they come with the villa but, everything else is ours. With the divine prerogative given children to play and live their games excluding all else we let that which is in us come out, and live it, sometimes teetering on delicious insanity. So, let me tell you what was once told pilgrims; kick off your sandals you've arrived ! I've been waiting years for such as you to turn up and play one or two parts I have in mind ... you can give us a matinee of "The Tale of the Changeling Prince" just as soon as you like. Like a marvel, a precious work displayed, certain of its worth.

ILSE: Here ?

COTRONE: A private performance. Whenever you like.

CROMO: His intention is that we should never leave of
                   course.

COTRONE: Why should you want to ? There's nothing there
                   for you in the real world.

QUAQUEO: That's right, stay.

MILORDINO: I've no objection ... stay.

DOCCIA: *(Dolefully)* I'd like to point out there are eight of
                   them.

LUMACHI: If you're asking me ? Right. Right you are ...

BATTAGLIA: It is a very lovely place.

ILSE: I see. Then I shall tour the play myself, those parts
                   I can't play I shall read. I'll tell the story.

SPIZZI: No, that won't be necessary, I'll stay with you Ilse,
                   we'll give it together ... I shall always stay with
                   you!

DIAMANTE: *(To the Count)* Yes, you can count on me as well.

COTRONE: I suppose you feel you have a mission ... ?

ILSE: To the end !

COTRONE: Oh dear. Can you not see that here the play will
                have its own life, be valued for its own worth ? It
                will glow with intrinsical light.

ILSE: It glows within me, but that isn't enough .. it must
                live for all men.

COTRONE: *(Saddened)* Poor little play, just as you rejected
                your poor sad poet's love so too will they piss on
                his poor little play for ever and ever ...

                        *Enter a disconsolate Sacerdote who couldn't find
                        anything he wanted to put on.*

SACERDOTE: I couldn't find anyth ...

COTRONE: What you all need most of all is a place to rest.
                Since you won't stay Contessa there are other
                things to suggest.

COUNT: What other things ?

COTRONE: Not now, tomorrow at first light, the start rather
                than the night, and not the dazzling day but the
                small light of dawn when things are seen clearly,
                dawn is future, dusk is memory and clairvoyance
                ...Tomorrow. *(He lifts his arm to show them into the
                villa and asks:)* Do you have a spare script, at all ?

                        END OF ACT TWO

ACT THREE

The Curtain rises.

Scene: The Armory of "La Scalogna". Italy. 1937.

An arsenal of equipment for the presentation of theatrical events. On or through the rear wall, drop, or scrim scenic delights may float and transform; dawn skies, white clouds blown by winds, soft green and gentle slopes of a mountain, trees, an oval pool, a spectacular seascape of fishing harbour and lighthouse.

There are musical instruments, a piano, a trombone, a drum. There are bentwood chairs of the type used by acrobats. There are puppets lolling in the chairs.

The puppets are: three sailors, two trollops, one old pianist with long hair, one foul woman who runs a café.

In the unnatural light - and the light is odd, subterranean but unearthly, without any obvious source - the puppets, though slumped, seem alive.

The sound of fleeing feet. The sound of pursuing feet.

Enter Ilse as if pursued. Enter Count as if pursuing.

ILSE: I want to get out! Outside!

COUNT: Ilse, why do you flee ?

ILSE: I want to GET OUT! Where are we now ? This light. It makes me feel sick, does it make you ... ? Where does it come from ? And what are they ?

                  Pointing at the puppets, up on her toes like a dancer, arms elegant, the body showing fear.

COUNT: Three Sailors, the Old Pianist, and the Foul Woman who runs the café, I think ...

ILSE: They're not real ... ? *(She nods.)* I gave him the script ! These are the parts we can never cast.

(Desperation) Oh God, how do I get out ... ?

COUNT: Why ?

ILSE: I want to leave.

COUNT: Where ?

ILSE: It doesn't matter where ... out, out !

COUNT: At night ?

ILSE: It isn't night. Is it night ... what is it ? That ghastly
            bed. You touched me in that bed, how could you ?
            I lay there rigid and you touched me ...

COUNT: Yes I know, I know, I am aware, silly bed, so lofty
            and - horrible.

ILSE: I lay there on that filthy old violet moth-eaten
            eiderdown ...

COUNT: A bed Ilse. It is a bed.

ILSE: Then sleep on it. I shall not.

COUNT: Please ...

ILSE: Not I !

COUNT: It will be worse outside, more frightening ... up
            there you're with me ...

ILSE: Yes. You.

COUNT: It isn't me, surely ?

ILSE: You follow me like a beggar.

COUNT: Oh ! Should I not be at your side ?

ILSE: I'm afraid of you.

COUNT: Why ?

ILSE: You look at me, watch me. You ooze timidity and
                supplication from your eyes ... you excrete it, your
                hands lard it ... I am sticky with it - I am smeared
                with it.

COUNT: *(Mortified)* I love you.

ILSE: Don't you just ! And don't you know just when to
                mention it when it is the last thing one might wish
                to hear. Of course it's just another form of money
                lending, usury.

COUNT: Usury ?

ILSE: Exactly, you've accommodated me now you wish
                to be paid back all you've lost - I expect with
                interest.

COUNT: Ilse ! That's unforgivable.

ILSE: Yes isn't it, and do you hope to solicit an apology
                from me ?

COUNT: I have lost nothing.

ILSE: Then what are you looking for in my eyes ?

COUNT: You've gone. I want you back.

ILSE: On my back.

COUNT: What a foul thing to say ! No. I want you as you
                once were.

ILSE: When was that, who was that ? Me ? Once ? Give
                me a clue what I was once ...

COUNT: Aren't you still ... my Ilse ?

ILSE: Listen to me speaking, the words I say, the way I
                speak, is that me even? I don't know. I can't be

sure of my own words, that the voice I hear is mine. What you say, other people, all noise is a hole made in deafness, all words pitched through are shrill and cruel ... spare me words !

After a painful pause the Count says:

COUNT: It's true.

ILSE: What is ?

COUNT: I am alone. You love me no longer.

ILSE: Is that true or is it nonsense ? I can't be without you so perhaps it's nonsense ... what might be a good idea pet is that you stop expecting, look somewhere else. You know I can only give love when it is not downright every-day every-minute beseeched implored-expected-wanted-needed thought-about flopped-for ...FEEL, don't think ... and do try to be reasonable about it as well and leave ME ALONE !

The Count waits for a moment and then asks:

COUNT: Am I not allowed to think of myself occasionally ...

ILSE: You say you only want others to be happy.

COUNT: ... just once in a while ? If I'd known ...

ILSE: I can't even remember how to feel sorry.

COUNT: ... your feelings would change.

ILSE: My feelings don't change.

COUNT: That isn't true. At first ...

ILSE: At first ! What did I feel ? And how can you be sure that what I felt, I would still feel if we were still feeling it, still there, still then, not gone, long gone ? *(Scratching at her body)* Do see what we are now ! My feelings don't change, they stay ... but do we know we touch ourselves even, is this my body ?

COUNT: That's why ...

ILSE: Why what ?

COUNT: Why I want you near.

ILSE: I am ... near ...

            Scratching herself still. The Count puts out a hand to stop her.

COUNT: You'll hurt yourself ...

ILSE: We can't go back.

COUNT: I can see nowhere to go.

ILSE: This man ... *(She flops a hand.)* ... here ... says he invents truth.

COUNT: How does that help ?

ILSE: Does he ? Dreams more real than we are ?

            The Count groans, shakes his head.

COUNT: Dreams are altogether different.

ILSE: No dream could be more absurd than this ... truth. That we are here. If one allowed oneself to be swept along with the sweet thought ... it could lead to ... lunacy ?

COUNT: I think we have been swept along by dreams for a long time now. After a long walk we've arrived. When we left our home, down the stairs to the car with dear little Riri in my coat do you think of her? Her white silky fur ? ... The servants cried.

ILSE: If you list all we've lost ...

                   *She picks, scratches at her body again, the Count
                   takes her hand, calms her, stops her.*

COUNT: List the crystal drops that lit the marble staircase
                   we descended so happy and eager and confident,
                   to find outside it was cold it was raining and a
                   black mist waited. We should have known.

ILSE: *(After a pause)* Nevertheless ... for all that's said
                   and done ... nevertheless ... this misery we have we
                   have bought for a great deal of money ... *(Wryly)*
                   ... it must be worth something.

COUNT: Are you now telling me Ilse what I am always
                   telling you ... that we should not be disheartened ?

ILSE: Yes I am. Yes, that's right. You are good ...
                   perhaps I can get some sleep now.

                   *Exit Ilse and the Count by the door through which
                   they entered.*

                   *Drum roll and trombone. One of the sailor puppets
                   seems to ask cheerily:*

SAILOR: Don't they make life complicated for themselves ?

                   Heads of the puppets jerk.

                   *Enter La Sgricia from a right upper entrance. The
                   puppet heads slump. La Sgricia walks to the centre
                   muttering to herself, knocking the puppets to their
                   knees.*

LA SGRICIA: Everybody kneel down, everybody kneel down,
                   everybody kneel ... *(She stands in the centre of the
                   stage and prays:)* Oh Angel come down, I have
                   seen you with your hundred soldiers pluck me up
                   take me up let me march with you to that glorious
                   place, take me up, pluck me up, sing songs of

peace I am weary ...

The Angel of the Century of God heard singing.
Then perhaps seen. The 100 Winged Troopers of
Purgatory riding through the air, their marching
song clear and strong, The Angel their captain on
a huge white horse, in breastplate and helmet of a
Knight of the Guard of Our Lord 1797.

ANGEL OF THE
CENTURY OF GOD: "In pace ! In pace ! Armed not with the weapons
of war but the falchions of Faith tucked shields of
Charity. In pace ! In pace ! In the stillness and
silence, it is God who flings open the door to him
who wavers, to him who wanders, the trumpet
calls Come rest in peace. Requiescant in pace for
ever more. In pace ! In pace ! In pace ! In pace ! In
pace ! In pa ... ... "

Exit La Sgricia with the Angel of the Century of
God and imagined files of cavalry. The music
thinner and softer, the chorus fading until only the
voice of La Sgricia is heard in the distance.

LA SGRICIA: *(Off)* "Come rest in peace. In pace ! In pace !
Requiescant in pace for ever more"

The puppets seem to sigh, part of the chorus
fading. With one movement they are jerked up and
dropped back into the chairs to slump faces up.

Enter Cromo backwards. He changes his face
throughout the following scene; sometimes his own
face, sometimes the Customer, or the Prime
Minister in "The Tale of the Changeling Prince".
He is listening for a sound, stopping and listening
again, and again as if clairaudient.

Enter Diamante from another place. She is in the
costume of the witch Vanna Scoma in "The Tale".
She has the mask of the character pushed back
over her head.

She stops Cromo with:

DIAMANTE: Cromo. There you are ! *(He turns to look at her.)*
              Who are you supposed to be ? I mean your face ...

CROMO: What about you darling ? Pull your mask down
              and look decent.

DIAMANTE: I don't wear a mask as the Lady of the
              Bedchamber, nor do you wear a red nose as the
              Customer - I do believe I swallowed a pin though.

CROMO: Oh dear, that's sad.

DIAMANTE: I can feel it ...

CROMO: Oh dear, that's very sad.

DIAMANTE: *(Her throat)*... here.

CROMO: If you're supposed to be the Lady of the
              Bedchamber ...

DIAMANTE: I was taking off my Bedchamber costume ...

CROMO: ... you're in the wrong frock darling ... you're got
              up as Vanna Scoma the witch ... *(As she looks down
              at herself he flicks her mask down.)*... and this is her
              mask ...

DIAMANTE: I can't talk.

CROMO: It's the pin.

DIAMANTE: I can feel it, here ... here !

CROMO: Did you put it in your mouth when you took it off?

DIAMANTE: What ?

CROMO: The Bedchamber costume !

DIAMANTE: I haven't ...

CROMO: Yes you have ...

DIAMANTE: *(Looking down, plucking at her sleeve)* Yes I have.
              And you've got the Prime Minister's nose on ...
              with the Customer costume. It's no good, I can't
              talk ... two pins ! I remember one, there was a
              rusty one in the dress, but I took it out, threw it
              away. I didn't put it into my mouth. I've
              swallowed two! Perhaps I dreamt the other one.
              Perhaps before I dreamt ... if I'm not in the Lady
              of the Bedchamber costume any more...

CROMO: Pricking of the throat ? Tonsils. You'll find they're
              inflamed with nasty little white spots ...

DIAMANTE: Will I ?

CROMO: You will ... soon as you look. *(Then cruelly)* You'll
              still have to go on, you lazy whore ... drop dead.

DIAMANTE: Drop dead yourself.

CROMO: It's a thought. With the life we lead only thing to
              do ... I shall consider it.

                            Enter Battaglia in terror.

BATTAGLIA: Oh God look ! Look look !

DIAMANTE: Oh God where ? Where where ?

BATTAGLIA: There, there! Gone now ... in the air ... in the wall
              ... horrifying.

CROMO: If you've seen something then I'm sure you're
              right for I have heard something.

BATTAGLIA: Was it awful ?

DIAMANTE: That's enough ! Don't try to frighten me I'm not a
              well woman and I'm running a temperature.

CROMO: No, it wasn't awful ... come here I'll show you ...

             Battaglia and Diamante would rather not, draw
             back from Cromo who wants to take them by the
             hand.

BATTAGLIA: No thank you ...

DIAMANTE: Please, rather not ...

CROMO: It was music.

DIAMANTE: Music ?

CROMO: Extraordinary music ... down the end of the
             corridor, come on, it's all right ... from the water
             perhaps in the well ... it was like that ... cool water
             ... you have to find ... the right spot ... *(Moving to*
             listen)... come here ... listen ... no ...

DIAMANTE: What sort of music ?

CROMO: Elysian. Well I thought so. I lost it for a while ...
             then just a phrase, then gone again ... too close ...
             then ... there it was ... is ! Can you hear ? *(He*
             positions them) Keep very still ... eh ?

             Subdued music. Their faces change as they hear it,
             ecstasy.

DIAMANTE: *(In spite of her fear)* It's ... lovely ... !

BATTAGLIA: It's not that Sgricia creature on her bloomin'
             organ is it ?

CROMO: It bloody isn't, not music like that ... that's straight
             from paradise, and ...*(He moves just a step, they*
             follow in line.)... now you hear it, now you don't !

             The music has stopped as they move. They move
             back again together exactly. The music is heard
             again. Then they step back and the music stops.
             Together they put out their right legs and slowly

> *step back and with their left legs up and slowly
> moving down listen for the music again. When
> they hear it, Battaglia and Diamante jump back
> in fright, tugging Cromo with them. The music
> stops.*

BATTAGLIA: Makes you go all to pieces doesn't it ... oooooogh !

              He shudders with fright.

DIAMANTE: It made me want to ... want to ... want to ... pee.

CROMO: It's not the only thing you'll hear, or see ... here.

BATTAGLIA: I know, I know ... that wall out there ... it moves.

DIAMANTE: How can it do that ?

BATTAGLIA: It can, it did ... I saw the sky, the moon and it was
              like ... well you've never seen moonlight like it, I
              haven't ... and there was that slut sittin' on a long
              stone bench - the Girl in Red with the daft smile -
              I could have counted every blade of grass it was so
              clear and a little flirt of a man came up to her ...

CROMO: The Quaqueo creature ?

BATTAGLIA: No. Not him. Someone in a thing the colour of a
              tortoise, a bell thing, a cape, like a bell, ever so
              clear, I could see he'd stained his face. He gave
              her a little case, it glinted, then he jumped back
              and hid and watched her to see if she would open
              it but she didn't. She just smiled with it on her lap.
              I could see her teeth between her lips, clearly ...
              saliva on them.

CROMO: You weren't dreaming ?

BATTAGLIA: No, love. Clear as you two.

DIAMANTE: It's not a dream then. I did swallow that pin then
              ... oh Gawd, Cromo ... oh oh.

CROMO: *(A sudden thought)* Stay in that position ...

                  Exit Cromo the way he came.

DIAMANTE: Where do you think he's going ?

BATTAGLIA: I think we just ought to stand very still, duckie.
                  (They do, arms out.) I saw somethin' move, out of
                  the corner of my eye, no don't look, it was one of
                  those friggin' puppets.

DIAMANTE: *(Reassuring herself)* I don't think so. I'm sure they
                  haven't moved an inch ...

                  Re-enter Cromo beaming with delight.

CROMO: That's all right then, we're not here ! Thought so.

BATTAGLIA: Eh ?

CROMO: Go on, go and have a look. Don't make too much
                  noise, you might wake yourselves up ... your
                  rooms darlings, go and see ... go on ... I did ... go
                  on.

                  *Exit Battaglia and Diamante. As soon as they are
                  gone one of the Trollops seems to say:*

TROLLOP: Took a long time for the penny to drop.

CROMO: Who said that ?

TROLLOP: I said that.

                  *The Trollop opens her legs as if slipping off the
                  chair, she is perched on the edge of the chair, her
                  skirts up. Cromo eyes the puppet, then lunges:*

CROMO: How do you do ?

                  *Re-enter Diamante and Battaglia to find Cromo
                  holding out the Trollop in front of him. Battaglia is
                  now dressed as a Trollop in "The Tale" himself*

but he seems not to be aware of it.

DIAMANTE: If this isn't my body, why can I touch it and feel it?

BATTAGLIA: I can too. I saw myself too.

DIAMANTE: *(Suddenly aware)* I am actually …*(She quakes with fear.)* … going to scream.

> *Cromo quickly puts his hand over her mouth, leaving his Trollop standing.*

CROMO: Don't scream. Don't …

BATTAGLIA: *(Nodding at the Trollop)* Look. I told you one moved.

> *Diamante opens her mouth to scream and Cromo holds the back of her head with one hand, his other hand over her mouth. She goes limp so that he is holding her up by her head, like a puppet.*

CROMO: We've woken up outside our bodies.

BATTAGLIA: Oh good.

> *A pause. It sinks in. Cromo lets Diamante go. She asks hoarsely:*

DIAMANTE: Tell me, you must tell me, are we dead up there ? I looked dead.

CROMO: Dead ! I was snoring sweetly and happily and in key.

BATTAGLIA: *(Disappointed)* I had my mouth open. I usually look like a little child at rest, so I've been told …

SAILOR: *(Derisively)* Like a little child !

BATTAGLIA: Who said that ! What's that … ?

DIAMANTE: Who said that ? One of them moved I saw it …

CROMO: It's all in the dream ... *(He waltzes into the arms of the standing Trollop.)*... we're asleep up there but here ... have a sailor ...*(He throws a Sailor into the arms of Diamante.)*... and you Battaglia, you're dressed like a trollop, enjoy it ...

            Another Sailor into the arms of Battaglia who staggers back and falls with the Sailor on top of him screaming.

BATTAGLIA: I don't want to do it ... I don't want to do it ...

            The Sailor appears to pluck him up and whirl him into a dance, so too Diamante who struggles but can't seem to free herself from her Sailor's clutch:

CROMO: It's all right, it's a dream, come on, dance ... it's in our dream all of it ... please ...*(To his Trollop)*... please ... a little slower I think, please ...

            Music.

            A very sinister dance. The Puppets who are never really alive nevertheless seem to control the movements of Diamante and Battaglia and even Cromo when he tries to stop on the entrance of Spizzi.

            Enter Spizzi with a length of rope.

SPIZZI: Let me through ..*(Through the dancers)*... I'm going to end it all.

            Cromo dances him round, asking:

CROMO: What with ... what with ?*(Holding up the arm of Spizzi and its dangling rope)* You idiot, it's a dream, you're hanging yourself in your dream.

            Spizzi tears himself away from the dancers, who try to laugh at him, but Battaglia is starting to sob.

SPIZZI: You'll see if it's a dream when I drop.

                   Exit Spizzi.

CROMO: And all for love of a Contessa !

                   Enter Lumachi and Sacerdote in dismay.

LUMACHI: Stop him. Stop Spizzi ... he's set on hanging
                   himself ...

CROMO: No he's not ...

SACERDOTE: Yes he is ...

CROMO: ... it's a dream.

BATTAGLIA: It's a ... it's a ... oh !

DIAMANTE: It's a dream ...

SACERDOTE: I don't dream.

CROMO: We're all asleep in our beds.

DIAMANTE: ... Spizzi's in his bed.

LUMACHI: No he isn't ... look ! He's hanged himself ...

                   *Imagined Scene: the soft green and gentle slopes of
                   the mountain, trees, an oval pool. A tree in the
                   foreground. Spizzi hangs from the imagined tree.
                   All shriek in horror and rush towards him, hitting
                   a wall just as lights fade swiftly to black, Puppets
                   and People intertwined. Cries of bewilderment and
                   laughter.
                   Gone.
                   Darkness.*

                   *Scene: the light comes back on. There is nobody
                   there. The Puppets are back on their chairs except
                   for one left lying near the wall twitching slightly.*

Enter Ilse, Cotrone, Count.

ILSE: I saw him ! Hanged from a tree.

COTRONE: There are no trees there.

ILSE: Where ?

COTRONE: Behind the villa.

ILSE: Yes, by the fish pond.

COTRONE: There is no fish pond.

ILSE: I saw the fish ... every scale and eye. *(To Count)*
             You saw it !

COUNT: Yes, yes I saw him. Hanged.

COTRONE: Calm yourself, Contessa. It's this place. It
             happens every night, the villa does it, fetches
             dreams, music, dreams, out of us. They don't
             have any coherence, only poets can do that ...
             look, he's here - the young man who started it
             all by dreaming he hanged himself.

             *Spizzi has entered while Cotrone has been
             speaking, as if still asleep. He wakes suddenly,
             offended, belligerent, asks:*

SPIZZI: How do you know ?

COTRONE: *(Placating him)* We all know it my dear chap.

SPIZZI: *(To Ilse)* You ?

ILSE: Yes I dreamed you did.

COUNT: I did. Same dream.

SPIZZI: How ?

COTRONE: You're so obvious, like all young men, even in your dreams which you seem to insist on sharing. It happens as the moon washes the earth life leaving it melancholy outlines, shadows and dreams come out and the more passionate amongst us tie a rope round their necks and go looking for a convenient branch of a convenient imaginary tree. We all talk too much old chap, too many words, and afterwards we regret, slink back into our kennels like dogs who've barked at nothing.

SPIZZI: Not my words. I speak the cursed words and feelings of another night after night, twice on Saturdays.

ILSE: Words addressed to a mother.

SPIZZI: He didn't think of you as his mother when he wrote the bloody words.

COTRONE: Oh come now my dear fellow, you can't blame the words of your part. It's never the words. *(He yawns, shivers, laughs.)* Not words. Speaking which, and of which: I think I know where you may perform your play. You see, dawn ? I promised you at first light ...

> *Imagined Scene: a dawn sky, white clouds blown by winds across it.*

ILSE: Ohhhh !

COTRONE: The mountain giants are the answer, they'll let you perform.

> *The Count is small and with his hand rising up above his head he emphasises his lack of height, asking:*

COUNT: Giants ?

COTRONE: Oh no not really, they're just trying to be, hoping to be, are very tall and muscular and fit and powerful and live on mountains in the fresh air like gods. Two of them are getting married, you must have seen it, in all the papers, Uma di Dornio and Lopardo d'Arcifa ? I'll arrange it. You have to watch your step with them, leave it to me because they are ... well the sort of work they do, you know, the intense concentration of physical strength and courage needed to fulfil all the tasks they have set themselves ... very hard work, dangerous, they take great risks every day of their lives building viaducts and aqueducts, factories, dams, roads, aerodromes, such wide roads and fields full of grain it's a tremendous success ... and, they're justly proud of their achievement and their muscles but it takes its toll this sort of thing and they are, sad to say, on the whole - thick as shit and twice as nasty. I find I can handle them. Pride. They respond to flattery. Let me do it for you. What's your get-out, would you like a guarantee or a flat fee ? We'll make it substantial they'll respect you the more if we do ... no, what I really want to know is how you're going to stage it?

SPIZZI: Haven't they built a theatre ?

COTRONE: They go in for stadiums. But that's no problem, we can put a stage up anywhere ... no, I spent the night reading the script, with my friends and I have to admire your courage, signor Conte ... it's a huge cast, and there are only eight of you.

COUNT: Yes there are a lot of characters.

COTRONE: Yes and they've all got lines.

COUNT: We've got the principals.

COTRONE: Yes that's not the problem. It's the magic.

ILSE: Yes, exactly.

COTRONE: How will you get it ? You can't hope to. It's a

choral work to start with ... I can see where the
money has gone. It's splendid. I was deeply
moved, captivated even. As I read it I knew that it
belonged here, with us ... where the reality of
fiction gives the body pallid nonentity.

The Count indicates the puppets.

COUNT: Is this what you offer ?

COTRONE: Me ? That was quick. I didn't know.

COUNT: Didn't you do this ?

COTRONE: No. It happens here. I told you, the place is ...
             haunted and as I read, so it happened. Not
             surprising. You surprised ? We're not, we're used
             to it. Human pride prevents us from accepting
             there are others on this earth living a natural life.
             We don't see them except perhaps when there is a
             flaw in one of our five very limited senses.
             Sometimes there are abnormal circumstances and
             we do see things and it scares us rotten, because
             we hadn't even guessed there were others not
             human who live amongst us not seen, spirits of the
             earth, rocks, woods, water, fire ... the air. The
             ancients knew and the common people have
             always known. We take them on here, curb them,
             and use them to give our work a significance they
             know and care nothing about. Should you still
             cling to the world of the possible and the natural,
             Contessa, you'll find things very bewildering here
             where imagination is given life, birth is
             spontaneous and easy. All that's needed is for our
             imaginings to be properly alive within us. The
             puppets are an example; if they are given the souls
             of the characters they dress to represent they'll
             move and talk ... it will simply happen, it's nothing
             ! Nothing that is, compared to the real miracle
             which is the invention of them by the poet, born
             alive in his imagination so that you can, as they
             say: "almost see them", even if they are only words
             on paper. That is what happens in theatres where

characters are born into a fictitious reality. Your job.

SPIZZI: So, we're the same as puppets are we ?

COTRONE: Oh no, they're much better. After all, the soul of the
             character actually inhabits them, and they are not
             ever anything else but that character.

SPIZZI: I'd be curious to see this ...

COTRONE: Then you won't. Curiosity isn't enough. You'll have
             to believe the way children accept and believe. The
             Poet whose play you tour imagined a mother who
             believes her baby son has been replaced by another
             stolen by witches called simply "The Ladies" - which
             seems ridiculous to educated people, you think it
             ridiculous perhaps yourself but, we know them "The
             Ladies" - they exist, we've heard them here on
             stormy winter nights, their shrieks on the wind. We
             can call them.

             "By night they come
             by the chimney
             like
             black
             smoke
             mother asleep
             exhausted from the day
             they stretch out the bones of their
             fingers ..."

ILSE: *(Perplexed)* You know it ?

COTRONE: Every word. We could do the show right here ... not
             for us, but for you so that you might see what we
             can give you. Try Contessa, see ... relive your part ...
             when did it happen ?

ILSE: What ?

COTRONE: Your baby was changed.

ILSE: Oh ... oh ...

(Snapping her fingers and closing her eyes she says:)
One night ... one night as I lie
sleeping I hear a cry ... I awaken
grope in the dark for my child.
(Then sings)
"Not there, not there
where ? where ?
Where is my child ?
Tight in his bands
He could not move
my child ! my ... ... "

She stops. Cotrone urges her on.

COTRONE: Go on ... the next line ...
              (He sings.)
              "Is it not true? Is it not true ?"

              *Ilse closes her eyes again and as she does so there is
              a change in the atmosphere and the light, it seems
              to hover, dim and then freshen into another kind of
              brightness, eerie and theatrical. With the brightness
              two women appear, one on each side of her, the
              two Neighbours of the first act of "The Tale of the
              Changeling Prince".*

              *Imagined Scene: the spectacular seascape of fishing
              harbour and lighthouse.*

              Cotrone still asking, "Is it not true?" is answered:

NEIGHBOUR 1: "True ! True !"

NEIGHBOUR 2: "A baby
              How could he ?
              Six months old ... ?"

              *Ilse, the Count, Spizzi react in amazement and
              fear.*

ILSE: Good God ... who ?

SPIZZI: How did they appear ?

COUNT: What's going on ?

Cotrone shouts, urges, like a director:

COTRONE: Go on, go on, keep going ... there's nothing to be
                worried about, surprised at ... you've brought
                them, they're here, keep them ... go on ... now say
                the next line, "When I gathered him up ... "

Ilse obeys, repeats:

ILSE: "When I gathered him up
                Thrown - there - under my bed ... "

From above in derision is heard:

VOICE: "Rubbish, the child fell. He fell !
                He fell !"

Ilse looks up in terror. Cotrone urges her:

COTRONE: Go on, go on, don't lose it, it's there in the play ...

ILSE: Yes.
                (She calms, then with total absorption she sings:)
                "He fell, he fell, he fell,
                It's said he fell
                They tell me he fell
                My child
                He fell, he fell, he fell !"

NEIGHBOUR 1:   "If he fell how did he fall ?
                Those who say he fell
                How did he fall
                Under the bed where he fell ? "

ILSE: "Tell them, tell them
                How was he found ?
                You who came to my screams
                Tell them, tell them ... "

NEIGHBOUR 1: "Turned ..."

NEIGHBOUR 2: "Feet to the head
of the bed ... turned"

NEIGHBOUR 1: "Tight wrapped
little feet
little hands and legs "

NEIGHBOUR 2: "Tied tight"

NEIGHBOUR 1: "Turned ... "

NEIGHBOUR 2: "He had been taken
a spiteful trick
placed under the bed
by hands ... "

NEIGHBOUR 1: "Not just spite
More than spite ... "

ILSE: "When I gathered him up ... "

NEIGHBOUR 1: "Such tears !"

*From above and around a terrible barrage of
incredulous laughter is heard. The Neighbours turn
to face the laughter and shout together:*

NEIGHBOUR 2: "We swear to it.
That child was
not the same
child. It was
another child. It
was a
changeling !"

NEIGHBOUR 1: "We swear to it.
That child was
not the same
child. It was
another child. It
was a

changeling !"

More laughter. Abruptly shut off with darkness.
Ilse heard in the darkness singing:

ILSE: "How he cried, my child,
               Not my child, how he cried.
               It was my child,
               Who cried ... my golden child"

               Chatter of the entrance of Cromo, Diamante,
               Battaglia, Lumachi, Sacerdote takes up the dying
               fall of Ilse's song and with their entrance comes the
               light.

CROMO: Did you call a rehearsal ? Am I called ?

DIAMANTE: I can only walk through it, my throat is in shreds.

SACERDOTE: Spizzi old man, thank God you're alive ... ! I don't
               dream, I never dream ...

BATTAGLIA: What's going on ?

LUMACHI: What is it ?

COTRONE: Contessa, you have just performed a scene from
               your poet's play with two characters who exist
               simply because of the power of His ... and your
               imagination.

ILSE: Where ?

COTRONE: Spirited away !

ILSE: Why ?

CROMO: Who ?

BATTAGLIA: What ?

COUNT: You know the play, you know the scene with the
               two women ... they came and did the scene.

SACERDOTE: Hardly ever ...

DIAMANTE: How did they ?

COUNT: They appeared. And did the scene.

CROMO: Who did the laughter ? I hated that laughter .. why
                weren't we called ?

SPIZZI: Tricks ! That's all ...

SACERDOTE: Yes ...

COTRONE: Not tricks ...

SPIZZI: Come on ... we're pros.

SACERDOTE: That's ri ...

COTRONE: That's as may be. If you were a real pro you
                wouldn't protest, you wouldn't look for tricks. You
                would, instead of giving way to more pressing
                personal interests have let yourself accept - as a
                child.

SPIZZI: We are not children any more, any of us.

COTRONE: Are we not ? If we ever have been we can be again.
                You had the face of a child when the two women
                stepped onto the stage and spoke. *(To the Count as
                well)* Both of you.

CROMO: That they did I accept. Now, how did they ?

COTRONE: As they were needed, and they spoke the lines ...
                isn't that enough ? Nothing else matters. This I
                wanted to show you, Contessa to prove to you that
                your young poet's work can only live here. *(A
                tremor of sound)* But you are urged on to give it to
                the world, the people, the public, so that's that
                ... *(Rumble of noise)* I can't do much for you out
                there, I have no powers, but I'm willing to try.

*The noise quickens, the ground trembles with it,
and there are shouts from off:*

QUAQUEO: *(Off)* The giants !

MILORDINO: *(Off)* Here come the giants !

The walls shake.

*Enter Quaqueo, Milordino, Maddalena, Doccia,
and Mara-mara, shouting excitedly:*

MILORDINO: They're marching down from the mountains !

MARA-MARA: Horses and men hundreds of them, columns of
them.

QUAQUEO: Listen to them ! Listen ! They rule the world !

*Music, harsh and martial, the clatter of steel and
squeal of tank tracks, roar of engines, sharp and
precise step of cavalry, strident brass, drums
thudding, shrieks of command, armoured columns
and people on the move in a triumphant assertion
of power. Over it all the ringing of church bells.*

MILORDINO: They're going to the church for the wedding.

Diamante excited and fearful.

DIAMANTE: Oh ! A wedding. Where can we see them ?

COTRONE: *(With authority)* No ! Stay where you are, all of
you.

COUNT: It's terrifying ... Ilse, do you hear it ?

*Spizzi, Sacerdote, Cromo and Diamante cluster
together as the walls shake and the savage noise
increases, Ilse calm in their midst.*

SPIZZI: The walls will come down !

CROMO: It's terrible. Savages ... the march of savages.

*They huddle together as the sound begins to fade
into the distance, down the mountainside. A
persistent flugelhorn causing a shudder each time it
sounds. The buccine of the Legions.*

END OF ACT THREE

ACT FOUR

Scene: on the Mountain of the Giants. Italy. 1937.

The sound of a lot of people assembled or assembling.
A Saracen olive tree and newly built futurist house of Paladini steamship
style. From the olive tree to the house is stretched a curtain. Beyond the
curtain is a vast open space which was at one time a Roman
amphitheatre; the stones still stand, and some of the seating remains
though a lot of stones have been used as foundations for the house. The tree
and the curtain and the house hide most of the open space from view and
darken the foreground. Above and through the curtain when lifted the sun
darts and dazzles and the amphitheatre shimmers like a mirage; a vast
open space full of people still eating and drinking in celebration of the
wedding of Uma di Dornio and Lopardi d'Arcifa.

The cart is under the tree and another curtain is pegged and looped from it
to form a tent for Ilse. There is a large cracked full length mirror propped
up against the cart. From the bowels of the cart, costumes have been
tugged and tossed onto the ground or convenient projections.

There is a tin bath, two or three large ewers full of water, towels. A lot of
food has been eaten, hunks of bread, fruit, cheese and clean picked bones
remain, piles of plates and serving dishes; bottles full and half full, glasses
with wine in them still. A trail of gluttony to the curtain and under it.

Discovered Cromo, Battaglia, Diamante, Sacerdote replete, giving the
occasional fart, belch, twitch. In costume they wait to go on.

Lumachi peering through the curtain.

Spizzi aloof, quiet.

Battaglia snorts nervously, a deep breath and snorting again says:

BATTAGLIA: I suppose you could say it's full, I've never seen a
fuller house.

SACERDOTE: Oh ...

DIAMANTE: That's something.

They all jerk nervously into their individual warm-ups.

CROMO: *(Yawning)* Did you see the one with the belly, the bursting shirt, the beard, the blood red nose, the bottle of wine on his knee ? He's going to love it, especially the quieter bits, you'll be able to hear a pin drop. *(To Diamante)* A pin drop.

DIAMANTE: Don't ... it still hurts.

She starts to do silent mouth exercises. Leans across to stretch a leg up like a dancer with her hand on the barre of Lumachi's shoulder.

BATTAGLIA: Not stingy at all about feeding us. I feel quite ill.

He looks in nausea and disgust at the detritus.

LUMACHI: They're clearing the best seats. I tried to. *(Diamante whispers in his ear. He ignores her.)* They wouldn't listen to me.

CROMO: That's something.

DIAMANTE: What is ?

CROMO: They intend coming. The Giants. The best seats.

DIAMANTE: Yes.

Spizzi gives a great sigh. Then in a high unnatural voice which startles says:

SPIZZI: This is the last time I shall play this part.

The others look uneasily at each other and at Spizzi who stands very still, relaxed but his fingers moving. Sacerdote moves towards him anxiously.

SACERDOTE: Oh ...

BATTAGLIA: He's been behaving very oddly.

CROMO: Why is this the last time ?*(To the others)* Why now?

DIAMANTE: I thought he was going to follow her for ever ?

SACERDOTE: *(Worried)* It isn't an intention, it's a premonition.

CROMO: *(Relieved* Oh good.

> *Enter the Count. He is flushed and excited.*

COUNT: All is well. The ... er ... Giants are delighted.
               Cotrone was an immense help. He explained to
               them who we were and that we could offer them
               something really ... really ... really ...*(He looks
               back.)*Yes, they have cleared the best seats, there
               will be quite a few of their skilled workers and
               artisans but they will be specially selected I am
               assured. They will behave themselves don't you
               worry, the Giants don't stand for any nonsense ...
               yes ... they really are the most ... charming people,
               they are in fact the Giganti family ... and I am sure
               ... appreciative. Lumachi ! As soon as the Giants
               have taken their seats and are settled, call the
               Contessa. Not a moment before. I shall go out
               front to wait for them. Welcome them. I think
               they'd probably like me to sit with them ... there
               may be a language problem but really I think jolly
               good ... ?

> *The Count smiles nervously, distractedly at them
> all and then goes back . The actors settle into the
> gentle warm up movements that they prefer.
> Cromo yawning a lot.*

DIAMANTE: Why will there be a language problem ?

CROMO: There always is.

SACERDOTE: Yes, oh yes ...

DIAMANTE: I know but why particularly ?

CROMO: Darling, they speak no known language, didn't
              you notice or were you too hungry to care ?

DIAMANTE: I was too hungry, and I never listen, what
              language is it here ?

BATTAGLIA: It's going to be awful. I've never seen the Count so
              happy, awful. Has he been drinking ?

CROMO: Have you ?

BATTAGLIA: Yes lots, pet. It hasn't made me happy.

SACERDOTE: Oh ...

CROMO: Didn't you find any little friends out there at the
              wedding ?

BATTAGLIA: Oh do piss off. No, I didn't. There was one chap I
              thought rather shy and nice. He'd seen a play
              once. Not here. He'd been a sailor.

SACERDOTE: Oh dear ...

CROMO: Of course he had. Where ?

BATTAGLIA: What ?

CROMO: Had he seen a play ?

BATTAGLIA: I don't think he had. I think he'd seen a Punch
              and Judy.

CROMO: Thank God for that, the cast of most plays for
              sailors consists of donkeys and whores ... I
              suppose we could find a donkey. Lumachi could
              do it. He has an affinity for donkeys, but has he
              the equipment ?

LUMACHI: *(Lighting his pipe)* I know what you think of them
              out there but they seem to me ... to be good
              people. Not very intellectual I'll give you that ...
              but good honest hard working folk who like a bit

of fun. Some of them are first class tradesmen ...
and craftsmen and ... journeymen who have served
their time, and they are very ... ... soft ... in their
own way. You only have to see the way a man uses
his hands ... the way he holds a piece of planed
wood ... to know that ...I would say ... that these
people is the salt of the earth. Or a tool ... or a
piece of stone. I look at these things. Salt of the
earth.

CROMO: That's that then.

LUMACHI: I think you'll be surprised.

BATTAGLIA: That's the most I've heard old Lumachi say in
years, he must have found a home.

CROMO: The Giganti family may not fully understand our
work but they will listen and they will receive us
with courtesy because they have pretensions. As
for their servants, salt of the earth they may be
Lumachi but from what I have seen and heard
they are not an audience for us. Those not sailors,
who have not been educated by exhibitions of the
tragedy of love in Port Said, Naples, Liverpool or
Marseilles are given to ribald songs and dances
bereft of any nuance or imagination and to do in
the main with those parts of the body which
vomit, excrete or accept the entry of familiar
unfamiliar even foreign objects. In-and-out - I call
them - songs, recitations and dances invariably
performed on the edge of tables. "The Tale of the
Changeling Prince" will not amuse them. We can
only hope that the presence of their masters will
temper their natural salt and earthiness.

A warning from Lumachi :

LUMACHI: Hey up ! Eyes down ..

*Enter Cuccorullo, a very thin civil servant
impeccably dressed and oddly sinister.*

CUCCORULLO: I am Cuccorullo. It occurs to me I should know
                   more of you and of your play. *(He waits.)* Who can
                   tell me about it ? *(Silence)* You ?

                   He points at Battaglia.

BATTAGLIA: Me, your honour ?

CROMO: *(To Battaglia)* What an extraordinary thing to call
                   him ...

BATTAGLIA: *(Whispering back)* What else, who is he ?

CROMO: *(To Cuccorullo)* I take it you are an official, a
                   minister ... ? *(Cuccorullo waits.)* Very well, I shall
                   break the habit of a lifetime because extraordinary
                   times make for extraordinary measures and talk to
                   you a member of the public, back stage ... *(In the
                   face of the implacable Cuccorullo taking notes, he
                   begins to falter)* ... before the performance contrary
                   to the ancient rules and usages and nature of this
                   theatrical art ...

                   A long pause and then Cuccorullo says mildly:

CUCCORULLO: I wasn't talking to you, I was talking to him ... you
                   are ?

BATTAGLIA: I know nothing, nothing.

CROMO: Say nothing. I fear the worst.

LUMACHI: They generally don't say much before the show,
                   get quite angry some of them if you say anything
                   to them, not all of them mind, some of them talk a
                   lot but not about anything, I generally ignore
                   them, just make sure they're in. She for instance
                   talks a lot, most of it dirty and suggestive - what he
                   does mostly is yawn, look at him - she has been
                   known to nibble my ear before we go up but if I
                   tried anything on I'd get short shrift, she's
                   warming up you see, relaxing you see, they try to
                   and they try to think of either nothing else or

everything else but their part or in this case their parts for they have several to do. But soon as she goes on she's coiled like a spring, ever so tense shoulders up here and she's lucky to get seven words in ten out which is how relaxed she is for all her flopping about and dirty talk. When we first started out on the tour I used to wear evening dress and white gloves ... I am by way of being the stage manager ... them were the days. Does that put you in the picture as it were, sir ?

Diamante is speechless and most unrelaxed with fury at the revelations Lumachi has seen fit to give. Cromo calms her.

CUCCORULLO: Where is the Contessa ?

LUMACHI: Ah, she talks to nobody. She opens the play you see and for three hours before we go up she says not a word so that the first words pass her lips are those of the play ...

SPIZZI: ... of the man she loves.

CROMO: I think it can be said, loved, excellency, she's devoted to the Count, excellency.

BATTAGLIA: There ...

SPIZZI: But she doesn't know the truth.

CUCCORULLO: What is the truth ?

SPIZZI: The truth is that the play is flawed.

CROMO: All plays are flawed, in the general sense that perfection is the prerogative of God, if one believes that is. I am apolitical, your honour.

BATTAGLIA: There ... I knew.

CUCCORULLO: It was banned in Berlin.

CROMO:	After the Chancellor had seen it and enjoyed it. He was persuaded afterwards by malicious untruth, I suppose - critics.
CUCCORULLO:	It was hissed in Rome.
CROMO:	The same applies.
CUCCORULLO:	What is the story of the play, you ?

Pointing at Sacerdote.

SACERDOTE: Me ? Er ... what can I tell you ?*(Cuccorrullo waits.)* Er ... a Mother, played by the Contessa has her golden haired son stolen in the night and another substituted, a nasty black and ugly thing. She is told she can do nothing about it because her own golden haired child has been taken to be the heir to the throne, the ugly black haired child becomes the village idiot, a cheerful enough creature but seriously mental, then the heir to the throne played by Spizzi here very frail and ill and translucently handsome comes to convalesce in the sun of the south. The poor Mother meets him and is certain he is her lost child, she tells him the story and the Prince discovers the love of his mother and would rather be poor but free in the sun. So that when the King dies, instead of going back he sends the ugly black idiot in his place to be King, and lives happily ever after poor but ... that's it really ... he would rather be poor but free with his Mother ... played by the Contessa brilliantly ... and as you can see there is nothing in it for either Herr Hitler or il Duce to object to, but ... I play the Priest, a small part, and others. We are the servants of of our art, actually, you must be told that ... all we care about, from the Contessa down to ... me. All we can do really.

CUCCORULLO: Thank you.

Cuccorullo who has been taking notes in a very small notebook with a very small pencil, spectacles on his nose, closes the notebook ...

SACERDOTE: Only way we can earn ...

... puts the pencil in its holder and looking at the actors all the time returns the notebook to his inside pocket. Then he goes.

Exit Cuccorrullo.

CROMO: Phhhhhhheeeewwwww !

Diamante screams in fury at Lumachi:

DIAMANTE: You cunt ! You absolute cunt ! How dare you tell him that ?

LUMACHI: It's true, and it's time it were said. You aren't no better than you ought to be ... you. And ... up go your shoulders ...

Diamante lunges at him. She stops short and turns her attention to Sacerdote.

DIAMANTE: And you, am I not in this play ? Can you not bring yourself to mention me, my role ... ?

She is silenced by a roar of triumph from the other side of the curtain, cheers, whistles, the sound of running feet.

Enter Ilse with her hands over her ears.

Enter through the curtain a Small Man in a best black suit too small for him, red tie round his ear. He grins nervously...

SMALL MAN: There's plenty of work here, good jobs too. Got to be fit though, it's hard work, worth it though, they look after you. Everybody is the same. There's nothing wrong with that. Do the job and earn the money, do good work and they appreciate it. Yes. Nothing's too much if a good day's work is done,

what's wrong with that ? You don't look as if
you've done a good day's work in your life ... is
that right ?

CROMO: I am an actor. I am not a manual labourer.

SMALL MAN: Please yourself.

CROMO: I will.

*... and then the grin fades to be replaced by an
attack of sheepishness which causes the Small Man
to scramble back to the other side of the curtain. A
cheer from the audience now filling the seats as the
Small Man finds his courage again and struts the
other side of the curtain, until pulled down. Another
cheer. Enter Count, horrified.*

LUMACHI: They're in the best seats.

COUNT: Ilse, they're savages ... they came down like, like
Huns, like ...

LUMACHI: They just come down and got in all the seats left
for the Giants.

Cromo at the curtain looking through exclaims:

CROMO: My God, Belly is in the front row.

LUMACHI: What is to be done now ? I can't get them out.

*Enter Cotrone. While he talks Ilse takes her hands
from over her ears. But she turns away from him
and responds to the noise coming from the audience
not to Cotrone.*

COTRONE: Contessa, Count, I have done my best and
thought I had persuaded the Giants but they now
say they must reluctantly decline the invitation.
They will pay for the performance of course, and
handsomely, that has been agreed but their work
which never ends even on holiday claims them,

they cannot now attend. They suggest you give the
play to the people.

CROMO: What ! That lot out there ?

Ilse has moved towards the curtain as if drawn.

COUNT: Ilse, you must not even think of it.

SPIZZI: She will. And I shall, with her.

*He begins to take off his clothes very carefully,
slowly, even ritualistically, folding everything,
making a neat pile, twitching folds to make the pile
square, symmetrical, his shoes on either side, like
the clothes of a recruit or a prisoner laid out for
inspection.*

CROMO: How much is offered ?

COUNT: It isn't a question of money, or you. I cannot allow
my wife to be exposed to that ... vulgarity ... that
... audience. *(He looks in horror at Ilse who listens to
the audience as if exalted)* Ilse ! A phalanx of
ignorance parades out there.

DIAMANTE: They terrify me but ... *(To the Count)* ... I'll go on
... if you wish us to, with her.

CROMO: They'll kill us.

COUNT: How can these wretches even begin to understand
the beauty of "The Tale" ?

COTRONE: How can anyone understand what it is that you
do? Or why you do it ? Separated only by that rag
of a curtain, are two groups of people who will
never understand each other. That lot out there
build and dig and slave for the Giants on roads,
monuments, bridges, magnificent pilings of stone
on stone which they spread before their masters.
With hearts full of pride a job well done, they
present the wealth of the world perfumed with

their sweat !

Their pride and purpose comes from an awareness
of the power and strength they allow their rulers.

They are ready to throw themselves gleefully at
any barrier, brave any odds fire, water, stone,
depth, height, weight, armies of enemies ... to that
end. Pride in achievement is individual and
collective and is their only goal.

Without fear of being overthrown, a settled state,
the Giants pay no heed to diversion ... music,
festivals, art. Their people have no knowledge and
no need. You might call them slaves and look at
them with contempt.

I doubt if they dream of anything.

And you here, this side of your shield, only a rag,
but it signifies, why are you here ? It isn't just the
weary urge to present your wares show the dreary
practice of your craft, your tricks of movement and
speech, your facility for mimicry, song and dance,
your insidious ability to enter the emotional life of
those persuaded to watch you. *(To Ilse)* You are
possessed by your poet, by your art.

You have trudged the world sustained by your
connection with another world - when starving
you have hoped it might sharpen your senses -
when rejected you have known it will stiffen your
resolve.

You are not like others, you have nothing to offer
in stone or weight, what you have - though you
have seen it once or twice - you have never caught.

Reality only exists for you in the words of a play
and your lives depend on it being so. You can hate
the poet and the art you are slaves to and wish you
knew how to live without either but, when you are
possessed by your poet you eagerly enter the

bodies of others without so much as please, shiver,
or thank you, shudder, potent with terror, sadness,
happiness, enlightenment, swooning delight,
whatever you care to counterfeit.

How will they understand you ? I doubt if they
even have a concept of Self - what impulses they
have they probably ascribe to voices in their heads
half heard quickly acted on in anticipation of the
wishes of their rulers.

They are willing slaves, they know nothing of the
tyrannous clutch of imagination. *(Urgently to Ilse)* I
saw you first when you were a girl and bursting
with joy. Come back with me to the villa where I
can look after you. *(To the others)* Free yourselves
by letting your imagination range without restraint
without any imperative other than true enjoyment.

Kick cowardly reason hence banish logic rid
yourselves of the debilitating urge to enter the
souls of others and, polish your own.

Refine your own lies, invent your own selves.

> *A steady chant going up from the audience the
> other side of the curtain. Ilse has hardly heard a
> word Cotrone has said.*

LUMACHI: She'll say nothing, she never does, no matter what
              we have had to face she has never said a word until
              that moment when she stands before them, alone
              on the stage ...

ILSE: I'm so tired of failure. It's so undignified. It's a
              land of half heard mutterings and apology. If we
              face this audience and make them listen then we
              have unbounded strength. We can measure the
              power of our sad young poet's play only by giving
              it to an audience like this.

LUMACHI: Well I never ...

ILSE: I feel that the simple beauty of his words will
                prevail.

SPIZZI: They will.

                *Shivering, he stands in the bath and pours water
                over himself. Sacerdote rushes to cover him with a
                towel.*

LUMACHI: *(In awe)* That's the first time she's said so much as
                ... so much as ...

                *As Ilse moves towards the curtain he starts to lift it
                for her.*

COUNT: Ilse, please.

                *He puts out a hand to stop her, she holds it and
                says to the others:*

ILSE: Promise me your best ... ?

DIAMANTE: Oh yes ...

CROMO: You have it madame.

                *Cotrone pushes himself between her and Lumachi
                and the curtain saying almost in desperation:*

COTRONE: If I went out and explained the story it might help.

ILSE: It's a wonderful story, beautifully told ...

SACERDOTE: Yes ...

COTRONE: They might listen. Let me ...

                *Cotrone ducks under the curtain. He is seen to
                raise his hands to a roar of welcome. He starts to
                speak: " The play you are about to see ..."*

                *Drowned by rattles, whistles, blowing of bugles,
                bang of drums and the figure of the Small Man*

seen up with Cotrone dancing round him.

ILSE: It doesn't matter.

She holds out her hand to Spizzi, face alight with fervour.

SPIZZI: I am ready.

CROMO: He can't go out there like that !

Re-enter Cotrone arms up and down in dejection.

COTRONE: I can do nothing.

CROMO: Leave it to me. If I told you some of the theatres I've played, what ... leave it to me. You have to soften them up, an audience like this, few gags, that sort of thing. *(His bravado fading)* I shall do my best ... *(He pulls down his nose.)* ... get some clothes on him.

Exit Cromo under the curtain. A roar of laughter and derision as Cromo is heard to say: "I'm the Prime Minister, you can tell I'm the Prime Minister by the size of my nose ... "

COUNT: Ilse, I beg you.

ILSE: What do you know of it ? Listen ?

Another roar of laughter greets Cromo and gradually builds to drown what he has to say:

CROMO: "My wife ... my wife I love her dearly ... very dearly ... she charges me for every ... kiss ... I'm saving up for a hug as well and when I get that I shall expect to be allowed to put my finger in her ... ear ... etc "

Drum rolls and cymbal crashes. Cromo seen - through the curtain - but not clearly heard for the din of the audience. Diamante and Sacerdote and

Lumachi begin to take some heart from Cromo's reception.

LUMACHI: That's all right, isn't it, that's all right ... *(To Spizzi)* Get your costume on young man.

Spizzi ignores him.

SPIZZI: The flaw is that this play was written for a base reason. Not for money, not for fame ... but for you, for lust ... that's why he killed himself, because he knew and that's why never until now has this play been true, no matter how hard we've worked, until now ...

ILSE: Why is it true now ? I know it is, I feel it is ...

COUNT: Please Ilse ...

ILSE: Go away ! You stupid man. *(To Spizzi)* You are right, but why is it now ?

SPIZZI: Now we risk what lives we have.

ILSE: Do we ?

SPIZZI: Oh yes, all of us. And now I don't love you more than I love the play. When I put the rope around my neck in my dream that part of me without hope died, I didn't know it until I felt the wonderful fear and hope of those voices, that ravening mob waiting to be subdued, tamed by the power of your art, and mine.

Lumachi gently, the tunic of the Prince in "The Tale" held in his hand:

LUMACHI: Here we are, put it on, lad.

SPIZZI: What's that ?

LUMACHI: Your costume ...

ILSE: No no ... he has it on.

SPIZZI: *(Dropping the towel)* Yes, it's linen. It's a suit of
                   faded and worn but well cut oatmeal linen, white
                   waistcoat, a silk shirt, straw hat and beautiful
                   shoes. Does that help?

ILSE: Made for you

SPIZZI: So comfortable.

                   *Cromo, the far side of the curtain, holds up his
                   hand:*

CROMO: No no the play you are. . . the play you are about
                   . . . the play we are about to . . . *(A jet of water hits
                   Cromo. Yelps of delighted laughter from the audience.
                   Cromo is thrown backwards through the curtain,
                   soaked and gasping. Roar of approval from the
                   audience who start to chant and clap, now impatient
                   for their next victim. "More more more" Cromo
                   gasping, trying to dry himself, and in spite of
                   everything curiously elated.)* I had them, did you
                   hear ? I had them. More, they want more.

                   *Cotrone at the curtain with Lumachi peering
                   through. The crowd chanting "More more more
                   more more more more more more ... "*

                   Ilse says Lumachi's name loudly and sharply:

ILSE: Lumachi !

                   *He holds up the curtain for her and for a moment
                   the others glimpse the audience, their open mouths,
                   their clutching hands, their cruel mocking eyes,
                   reddened by the the sun starting its rapid descent.*

                   *Ilse goes through, the curtain is dropped, there is
                   terrible silence.*

LUMACHI: What is art unless it is in the breast of every man ?
                   I know, for I was such as these myself until

captivated by its sweet and heady scent - though mind I did always have my head stuck in a book.

COTRONE: Shhhhhhhh.

CROMO: She's done it.

DIAMANTE: My God, they're going to listen.

SPIZZI: *(A sigh of exultation)* Yes.

SACERDOTE: And so they will, and so they will. We are those who will show them there is more to life than than ... than ... there is the spirit there is the life of the spirit all hope is in the spirit. We know what there is, we know what we have, we offer it ... and if it be scorned, so be it - it is the ignorance of slaves scorns it.

SPIZZI: Yes ...

COTRONE: They see you as puppets, they listen to your incomprehensible words, watch your serious strut and wait for the first small sign that you are as they ... when relief will come in laughter or sympathy or not.

> *Silence.*
> *Ilse seen the other side of the curtain, the silence becoming unbearable. The Count sobs from the tension and falls to the ground in a faint. No one moves to him, all are held by the silence. Ilse starts to sing:*

ILSE: "Listen to me.
Listen to what I have to say.
Look at what I wear.
See the truth of my rags.

As true as my pain,
my sighs.
I cry
as a mother cries.

The pain of a mother.
The grief of a mother."
(Laughter from the actors this side of the curtain,
strange, apprehensive, cued by Lumachi, each actor
their own laugh.)
"How they laugh,
you hear them ?
the clever people,
how they laugh,
at my simple tears
and are unmoved ..."

A loud and weary YAAAAAWWWWW–
NNNNNN ! from a wag in audience and the spell
is broken. Through the curtain to cries of encour-
agement from the audience the Small Man is seen
to caper onto the stage. The Audience shouts:

AUDIENCE: What's she talking about ? Who's she think she is ?
              Sing ! Dance ! Send out another one do do do do
              do do do ! More more more more more more ...

              Ilse seen through the curtain trying to continue, her
              voice heard trying but failing to compete.

ILSE: "More ... more ...
              .... furthermore,
              in their anger they cry:
              Fool ! Fool !
               her born son,
              impossible !
              her born child .... it cannot be !"
              (Figures of the Audience, huge, menacing and
              grotesque seen up on the stage, clambering up, shaking
              the flimsy structure. They seize Ilse by the waist, dance
              her from one to the other to roars and screams of
              delight. The stage shakes, the curtain is buffeted and
              all this side of it are aghast. Ilse still trying to be heard,
              fighting them off, shouting:)
              "Hear me,
              hear the witness of others,
              mothers,

poor mothers like me,
of my village,
of my life
they testify ... "
(Ilse seen to be lifted she screams and fights.)
You brutes, you foul brutes ... !

> *Spizzi groans and goes through the curtain, arms up as if entering water. Huge figures seize him. Cromo shouts:*

CROMO: Dance, dance, everybody get up on the stage and dance ... my wife ... my wife likes to dance ...

> *Cromo, Diamante, Lumachi and Sacerdote duck under the curtain and are swallowed up by the figures.*
>
> *Great fists are raised and come down, one, two, three, the thuds are audible. The screams of Spizzi and Diamante are heard as they are torn apart.*
>
> *Cotrone goes through.*
>
> *There is a burst of machine gun fire followed by silence and groans and sobs. The figures on the curtains are gone. The sun flicks a last red shaft into the sky, black clouds obscure it.*
>
> *Silence.*
>
> *Ilse is brought back by Lumachi, Sacerdote, Cromo, crouching in fear, stunned by what has happened. They drag her down through the curtain, and whisper urgently:*

LUMACHI: She's broken ...

CROMO: Ilse ... Ilse ...

SACERDOTE: Oh, not dead ...

> *Re-enter Cotrone. The actors cower in fear until*

they realise who it is.

CROMO: I don't think she's dead.

SACERDOTE: Did you see what they did to Spizzi, Diamante ?

LUMACHI: *(Hoarsely)* They tore them apart ...

              *Cotrone holds Ilse up. She tries to speak, fails, then
              manages ...*

ILSE: Invent this ... differently.

              *. . . and dies. The Count recovering consciousness
              as she does. He cries out in anguish and scurries to
              her, takes her from Cotrone, cradles her.*

              Enter Cuccorullo. The actors scatter.

CUCCORULLO: This is dreadful. Quite dreadful. We will fix the
              blame and punish.

COTRONE: There is no blame.

              The Count screams:

COUNT: So mankind destroys the work of the poet ... !

COTRONE: No. So, arrogant slaves of art are destroyed by
              uncomprehending slaves of life who see you as
              puppets, strutters, unable to speak to them. *(To
              Cromo)* You exclude yourselves from life at your
              peril. Dream your dreams but never ever try to
              impose them. There is only one place you may live
              your dreams and that is with me - I offered it you.
              (To Cuccorullo) Like others who have seen their
              play and - after their minions have whispered and
              destroyed their pleasure - struck at them in anger,
              you are a man frightened of poetry but, with its
              destruction I suspect you have begun its victory ...

CUCCORULLO: I am allowed to offer restitution.

COUNT: Restitution ! Restore me my life !

CUCCURULLO: There will be compensation.

Exit Cuccorullo.

COUNT: Ohhhhhh ... how can you ?

COTRONE: Take it. Take what he offers. It's over.You all
                    know it's over now that frail body is broken ...
                    I saw her first in "La Dame aux Camelias". I shall
                    never forget her secret sweetness - she
                    overwhelmed me with it, and the passion she
                    brought.

                    *(To the Count)*Use his money to build her a tomb.

COUNT: It shall be a monument to her and to Poetry.

COTRONE: Please yourself.

                    Why not ? But I shall not weep for poetry, I would
                    not die for it.

                    Accept the relief that floods over you now she is
                    dead. You may go back to being little men. The
                    urge you had will haunt you no longer.

                    *He bends down and takes the limp hand of Ilse
                    while Lumachi and Cromo and Sacerdote lift her,
                    put her on the cart.*

                    Exeunt omnes. Ilse on the cart as she came.

                    *But Cromo lags behind and is quickly back. He
                    clambers up onto the stage, holds up the curtain
                    and looks out at where the audience were. The
                    amphitheatre seen.He drops the curtain and starts
                    to pace. The creak and sway of the stage showing
                    his gradually building enthusiasm.*

                         THE END